♦ HOW TO ROCK CLIMB ♦

Big Walls!

John Long
John Middendorf

CHOCKSTONE PRESS
Evergreen, Colorado

Cover photos:

(front): Xaver Bongard floating in a Sea of Dreams, El Capitan; photo by Bill Hatcher

(back): Great Trango Tower, Pakistan; photo by Ace Kvale

ISBN 0-934641-63-3

Published and distributed by
Chockstone Press, Inc.
Post Office Box 3505
Evergreen, Colorado 80439

also in the
How to Rock Climb Series:

How to Rock Climb! by John Long
Sport and Face Climbing by John Long
Climbing Anchors by John Long
Knots for Climbers by Craig Luebben
Gym Climb! by John Long
Clip 'n Go by John Long and Duane Raleigh
Nutrition for Climbers by Beth Bennett
Advanced Climbing by John Long and Craig Luebben
Flash Training! by Eric Hörst

Acknowledgements

First and foremost, thanks to John Long, for his suggestion to work together on this book, and whose writings, additions, and editing transformed the dry technical how-to approach to describing the complicated systems of big wall climbing to entertaining, informative, and readable text.

In writing of the technical systems of big wall climbing, it is inevitable that many of the systems and solutions described are just one of many ways to make progress on the vertical. Knowledge of techniques have improved over the years. Each generation of wall climbers utilizes the previous generation's knowledge and improves and devises the next level of sophistication. Ever since Royal Robbins came up with the efficient idea of hauling gear through a pulley and mechanical cam system, the knowledge and beauty of methods of ascending large chunks of stone for many days with a ton of gear has grown. By no means is this book an exhaustive study of all possible big wall systems. The purpose of this book is to describe a complete, workable system that has proven to be efficient in climbing big walls. It is based on many years of big wall experience by the authors.

It is impossible to acknowledge all who have had an influence in the techniques described herein. Ever since my first big wall with John Ely, the Northwest Face of Half Dome, in 1977, I have learned many new or different ways of doing things on each of the 80 some-odd big-wall routes I have done since. Many times I learned from seeing how a partner with a different climbing backround perform the same task with a different method, and many times from devising a system on the spot to deal with the particular problem on hand. Regardless, I always understood that there was no single ultimate best way to wall climb. All it took was an open and imaginative outlook on creating solutions to difficulties. Ultimately, the only way to really learn the ropes on big walls is to go out and do it (and not from reading a manual such as this).

It would be impossible to acknowledge every source of techinique described in this book. But to name a few of the people whose spirit, techniques, and philosophy were sources for my writing is in order. For example: Werner Braun, who taught me cleaner climbing techniques and who with his hearing difficulties proved to me that it is possible to communicate effectively on big walls without verbal communication. Alex Lowe for opening my eyes to quicker methods of ascent, Walt Shipley for determination (and the entertaining post-wall "Walt shows"), Dave Schultz about taking chances, Mugs Stump about commitment, Steve Quinlan for many discussions of what the whole damn purpose is anyway, and last but the most importantly, to Xaver Bongard who was a natural master of big wall climbs, and taught me that perfect synergy between partners made extreme ascents possible. And to all the others who I've actually gone out and done a big wall with: Steve Bosque and Mike Corbett, Hideataka Suzuki, Derrick Hersey, John Bachar, John Barbella, Russ Walling, Charles Cole, Chuck Wheeler, Thom Englebach, Lydia Bradey, Eve Tallman, Jeff Hollenbaugh, Steve Chardon, Rich Albushcat, Jimmy Dunn, Eric Kohl, Rick Lovelace, Barry Ward, Conrad Anker, Stan Mish, John Wason, Will Oxx, Brad Quinn, Bill Hatcher, and to all the others.

Finally, but by no means least of all, I want to thank John McMullen for the many fine illustrations seen throughout the book.

John Middendorf

WARNING: CLIMBING IS A SPORT WHERE YOU MAY BE SERIOUSLY INJURED OR DIE

READ THIS BEFORE YOU USE THIS BOOK.

This is an instruction book to rock climbing, a sport which is inherently dangerous. You should not depend solely on information gleaned from this book for your personal safety. Your climbing safety depends on your own judgment based on competent instruction, experience, and a realistic assessment of your climbing ability.

There is no substitute for personal instruction in rock climbing and climbing instruction is widely available. You should engage an instructor or guide to learn climbing safety techniques. If you misinterpret a concept expressed in this book, you may be killed or seriously injured as a result of the misunderstanding. Therefore, the information provided in this book should be used only to supplement competent personal instruction from a climbing instructor or guide. Even after you are proficient in climbing safely, occasional use of a climbing instructor is a safe way to raise your climbing standard and learn advanced techniques.

There are no warranties, either expressed or implied, that this instruction book contains accurate and reliable information. There are no warranties as to fitness for a particular purpose or that this book is merchantable. Your use of this book indicates your assumption of the risk of death or serious injury as a result of climbing's risks and is an acknowledgement of your own sole responsibility for your climbing safety.

Dedicated to the memory of
Xaver Bongard

Preface

BIG WALLS!

JOHN LONG
JOHN MIDDENDORF

No precise definition exists that automatically qualifies a cliff as a "big wall," but any chunk of steep rock 1,200 feet or higher is certainly a candidate. In climbing parlance, a big wall's generic definition has changed a little as the sport has evolved. When big wall climbing was first established in the United States (in Yosemite Valley during the late '50s and early '60s), "big wall" came to mean any climb requiring predominately artificial techniques to ascend, and that required two or more days to complete. A select few big walls have been free climbed over the last fifteen years, and certain popular routes are now climbed in one day; but the old definition of big walls – a multi-day, predominately artificial climb – still holds today.

As opposed to free climbing – the gymnastic endeavor of scaling the rock using hands and feet – "artificial," or "direct aid" climbing entails the mechanical, mentally taxing and sometimes perilous task of ascending steep rock via strings of weight-bearing equipment fitted, slotted and hammered into the rock. The means and systems of rigging this equipment makes up the art of direct aid, or artificial climbing. Though it is the rare big wall that does not feature *some* free climbing, the hallmarks of a classic big wall remain vast sections of rock so steep and so sparsely featured that artificial techniques are the only means to ascend them.

Big Walls! is a practical, illustrated guide for someone aspiring to go out and put up a new wall climb on one of the mightiest cliffs on the planet.

Say, what?

Most climbers have no such plans, and never will. Many simply want to learn a little about aid climbing, should they ever get pressed into needing it. Others might aspire to do the D7 on the Diamond, Longs Peak, Colorado, a standard Grade V. Still others want to bag the Nose route on El Capitan, the most famous rock climb in the world, or a harder route still – on the Dru, near Chamonix, France; on some ghastly desert tower; on Mars, for that matter. Everyone brings different needs and dreams to a book like this, and few are looking to establish a blockbuster new wall climb at the end of the world. They want to pick up a few new tricks, refine their methods, review the latest gear and techniques, read a couple of anecdotes for sure. But never mind that blockbuster business.

That's just as well from our viewpoint, because learning a bit about aid climbing, scaling the Diamond, then the Nose, and so on, are all vital steps toward putting up that end-all wall on Trango Tower or Cerro Torre. This is precisely the route we'll follow: starting small, and working our way up, first with the basics, later with the trickier stuff, and finally with the perilous game of tackling a full-blown test piece on one of the planet's great rock walls. We can't claim to have done a complete job of it once we're on top of El Capitan, because Patagonia is waiting in the wings, and there are strategies to that arena that you'll likely never need on the "Captain." If you choose to bail after learning that little bit of aid technique, or after getting up the Diamond, or any pitch short of the end-all wall, that's your call. But there will be no retreating here till we've got you racked up and standing at the base of Cerro Torre. Then you're on your own.

There's no sense in trying to suggest what caliber of climber can most benefit from this manual, but unless you have a working knowledge of fifth-class climbing and are competent in all of the standard procedures, aid climbing is best put off till your fundamentals are solid.

I know the process of getting familiar with the climbing game. As a sixteen-year old novice, I (J.L.) read everything I could beg, borrow or steal on the subject long before I could understand it. No harm in that, for it gives a climber a glimpse of the farthest horizons. But going out and trying some aid climbing before you have belaying down cold, for instance, is simply not the way to go. As a rule (though not a definitive one), a year's free climbing experience is ample to go ahead and pursue a little sixth class work. But every case is different. For boning up on the basics, check the other books in the *How To Rock Climb Series*. This book is not introductory material, and it assumes you understand the substance of the previous books.

Although the art of free climbing is universal, climbers' techniques vary considerably from country to country. Most groups have arrived at rigging techniques tailored to their own rules and the vagaries of regional rock – say, using twin eight-millimeter ropes for leading rambling sea cliff climbs.

This is in sharp contrast to big wall climbing. Although the nature of different cliffs might vary considerably, the actual means of getting up all big walls remains ninety-nine percent the same for any rock, anywhere – on Half Dome in Yosemite, on Mt. Asgard in the Baffin Islands, on the Dru in the French Alps, and so on. So the techniques laid down in this manual are precisely the ones universally accepted by virtually all experienced wall climbers. These techniques evolved out of the golden age of wall climbing in Yosemite Valley in the 1960s, and were further refined with the advent of new gear and the new experiences of climbers venturing outside the relatively "safe" confines of the valley. So (much more than with any manual in this series), *Big Walls!* presents universally-accepted techniques and equipment be you American, German, Chinese or Swedish. It's all the same stuff on the high crag.

C O N T E N T S

1: THE VERTICAL WORLD 1

2: GRADES AND RATINGS 9

3: PLACEMENTS 15

4: AID SLINGS & WEIGHTING PLACEMENTS 27

5: LEADING 37

6: FOLLOWING PITCHES 47

7: MULTI-PITCH ROUTES 59

8: HAULING 69

9: MULI-TDAY ROUTES 81

10: ADVANCED AID TECHNIQUES 95

11: FIRST ASCENTS 103

12: SOLO TECHNIQUES 105

13: STYLES AND ETHICS 109

APPENDIX 1: YOSEMITE CLIMBS 121

APPENDIX 2: GEAR CHECKLIST 123

APPENDIX 3: CLIMBING AREAS 125

APPENDIX 4: SUPPLIERS 127

APPENDIX 5: GUIDES 128

GLOSSARY 129

BIG
WALLS!

JOHN LONG
JOHN MIDDENDORF

The Vertical World

I (J.L.) had just started college when I first began spending summers in Yosemite Valley. By the time classes let out in June, the valley was scalding and most American climbers had migrated fifty miles north to Tuolumne Meadows, where the climbing was good and the days cool. But the valley had the famous climbs, the big climbs, so I stayed there, often tying in with Europeans who welcomed the heat and the long Yosemite routes.

During my second summer there, I teamed up with British ace Ron Fawcet, who was probably the finest free climber in Europe, and would be for a decade to come. We were both nineteen, principally crag climbers looking to extend our repertories. We'd been climbing together for some weeks, doing short, hard free climbs, and feeling pretty good about ourselves; but every time we passed El Cap, we'd glance at each other like thieves because the amplitude of that rock, and the towering challenge it presented, totally overshadowed the silly little routes we were bagging.

So long as we pursued the dream, we felt we were dangling on the lip of heroism; but we were doing neither on the short routes. The dream was not 150 feet high. It was a mile high and profoundly dramatic. The short routes were exciting, but excitement was a poor substitute for the theater of doom found on the big walls – and we both knew it. One day at Arch Rock, we were both lacing up for a grim route that was barely a rope-length long. I looked up at it, started laughing and said, "What are we doing cocking around on this pissant climb?" The shorties all at once seemed like a game of charades, a surrogate ritual for our rendezvous with the heart of the dream. There was no more putting it off.

The next day we climbed a long route on Middle Cathedral Rock – or started to. We gained a big ledge after a couple hundred feet, and spent the rest of the day looking across at El Cap – just opposite – eyeballing the various routes and talking about trying it "one day."

This was tricky business, working on the fringe of the Big Question: when do we go for it? Physically, we knew we could do it. But pondering that mammoth chunk of granite it's your mind, not your body, that shudders. We intently listened to each others' voice, studied each others' eyes, trying to reckon without asking how the other guy truly felt about it. It's a known fact that you can't look at El Capitan

Northwest Face of Half Dome, Yosemite National Park.

George Meyers photo

and lie at the same time, not about wanting to climb it anyway. So we didn't press each other, afraid the other guy might be on shaky ground and try to lie, or start mumbling excuses about why he didn't want to climb it when you knew damn well he did. He had to, or he was a coward and an outright fraud. By the end of that day on Middle Cathedral, the Big Question had grown and swollen between us like a great festering boil. We'd have to lance it with the Big Answer if we wanted to continue as partners.

"Maybe we should have a go at it," Ron finally offered.

"Before it grows any more," I said.

There is a ritual all climbers perform before a long climb, and it hasn't changed much since "gentleman mountaineers" plowed up Mt. Blanc in tweeds and hobnailed boots two hundred years ago. The ritual flows from the fact that the quicker you get through the formalities and onto the route, the less chance you have of changing your mind; and after hauling Harding's epic through my brain a thousand times, I wanted to put that all aside and get on with it. Big climbs are not casual business, not something done for the fun of it, and there are always ready reasons why not to go. So when the urge strikes, you move on it.

Love that big wall gear!
Dan McDivett photo

The ritual goes like this: first, you pick the route, then a partner. Then you both go down with binoculars and study the climb. A wall veteran can tell much by a good glassing; a rookie can only get scared. The devil may show you a little flea of a man on your route, half a mile up, floundering and flailing and hardly moving at all. You picture yourself in his boots, glance at your partner, and go to the bar to drown the urge – if anything's left of it. If the urge is still kicking, you return to camp, spread a tarp out and, referring to the guidebook and any tips you've picked up from friends or acquaintances who have climbed the route, you set about organizing the mountain of gear.

Dozens of pitons are lined up side by side, according to size, like keys on a xylophone. Nuts are arranged, carabiners linked and counted dozens of times, slings tied and retied, ropes inspected, water bottles taped and filled. Then you stand back and stare at the gear. Then you stare at your partner. Then you go back and stare at the route some more. If you can still look your partner in the eye, you'll probably go through with it, return to camp, pack all the gear and the food into the haulbag and try to knock off early. And anybody who says he slept well, or at all, before that first big climb is either crazy or a liar.

We slithered out of our sleeping bags around four-thirty in the morning, and hiked to the base in the dark. The waiting before a big climb is harsh, but hiking to the cliff is the worst part of all. A few climbers are loud and won't stop yakking because the worm is turning hard and deep and their balls are up in their throats. Most are stone-faced and sweating the big drop. But the cliff, once gained, which you vicariously know so well, eases the stress and loneliness of the march. We started up at first light, hoping to get far up the wall that first day. The normal time needed to ascend the Nose was three to four days; we brought food and water for a day and a half.

From the start, Ron and I climbed like madmen, trying to quickly get ourselves so irreversibly committed we couldn't retreat, so the only way off was up. Up to that day, my typical climbing outing involved driving out to Suicide Rock or Joshua Tree National Monument, cranking off a couple gymnastic, picayune routes, then retiring to MacDonald's for burgers and enormous talk. But El Cap was commitment with a capital C, and like most newcomers to the high crag, part of me kept yelling: "Get the hell off this while you still can." It was simple inexperience talking. And it didn't help that the ground kept getting farther away, but the summit didn't seem to get one inch closer – an optical illusion particular to all big climbs. The secret is to stay focused on the physical climbing. If you simply cannot manage the climbing and exhaust yourself trying, fair enough. An honest failure never haunts you because the body knows no shame. But if you let your mind defeat you, if you bail off because the "vibes" are weird and you let fear run away with itself, you have not truly failed, rather defaulted, and it will nag you like a tune till your dying day – or until you return and set things straight.

At the 600-foot mark we gained the first big pendulum – a wild running swing right to the "Stoveleg Crack" (so named because on the first ascent, Harding nailed it using four crude pitons forged from the legs of an old stove scavenged from the Berkeley city dump). From the top of a long bolt ladder, you lower down about 60 feet, then start swinging back and forth. Now at speed, you go for it, feet kicking hard, digging right. You hurtle a corner, and as you feel the momentum ebbing, you dive. If you've chanced it right, you plop a hand into a perfect jam just as your legs start to swing back. You kip your torso, kick a boot in and you're on line. A laser-cut fracture shoots up the prow for 350 feet of primarily perfect hand-jamming, the wall as smooth as a bottle and not a ledge in sight, each lead ending in stark, hanging belays. The climbing went quickly and by noon, we were on El Cap Towers, a perfectly flat granite patio about twenty by six feet.

This was our first chance to catch our breath and take stock of our situation, racing as we'd been just to get there. I peered up and across and straight down, and images were thrown back that no climber can entirely fathom and no one in any language can do justice. "Holy fucking mackerel!" I yelled. What a strange mingling of terror and exhilaration I felt gazing down at the miniature buses and cars creeping over a world we'd left only a few hours before, but from which we were now separated by a distance that could not be measured by any yardstick. I flashed on my friends in Camp 4, half of them foreigners, and marveled how the dream extended beyond local or even national interests, and how much more outrageous the deed was than the idea of it. If it entailed physical dangers, I reasoned, surely they were worth facing. But there was no explaining away the shocking uneasiness of facing the distance outright.

Above the comparatively low-angled Stovelegs, the upper wall rifles up into perfect corners – like a cut melon. Out to the right looms the fearsome sweep of the southeast face, which at dawn draws fabulous hues into its keeping. There lie the world's most notorious big wall climbs, and it's hard to imagine an arena where man has fewer claims and less authority. We were following a good, secure crack system, but no such thing lay out to the right. No ledges, no ramps. Nothing but a chilling, 95-degree wall, a shadowy void damn scary to even look at. Since Royal Robbins, Chuck Pratt, Tom Frost and Yvon Chouinard first scaled it in 1964, via the North America Wall, a dozen other routes had been established thereon; and what epics this great sprawl of granite must have witnessed. From our ledge on El Cap Towers, it seemed we could hear the echoes of all the tense leaders who had once passed there – their terrors and doubts, hooking and bashing their way up the wall's overhanging immensity. And it seemed, too, that we could see their moon eyes glaring at belay bolts hanging half out of the gritty diorite bands, where a dropped piton strikes nothing but the ground half a mile below. A precious few specialists thrive on this kind of work, and they make the most curious study in all rock climbing.

We pushed on, traversing up and across the Grey Band, a nebulous stretch at mid-height that follows an intrusion of flaky ash monzonite. By early afternoon we'd reached Camp Four, a small recess of puny terraces below the final corner, which soared straight to the top, 1,200 feet above. Suddenly, the breeze died, and the cruel heat welling off the white rock stopped us dead. The next ledge was 500 feet higher, so we decided to bivouac right there, on Camp 4.

Pancake Flake pitch, The Nose of El Capitan

Bob Gaines photo

No longer absorbed with hauling bags and climbing hard and fast, the bivy was like suddenly finding ourselves becalmed after a typhoon. We dropped anchor, clasped the rigging, gaped up and down and every which way, trying to get our bearings. We studied the topo map to reckon where we were, and what lay between us and the home port on top. We tossed off some small talk, sipped the precious water, nibbled sardines and cheese and tried to ignore the fact we were marooned on a knobby, down-sloping ledge scarcely big enough to sit on, 2,100 feet up the side of a cliff, with 1,200 feet of heavy weather overhead. Exhausted, we eventually laid back and tried to settle in, rattled by the naked feelings dancing through our heads.

If wall climbing is good for nothing else, it's a sure way to find out, once and for all, how you really feel – not what you're expected to feel, or have been told or taught to feel. Slowly, you take on the stark, naked aspect of the great wall, and sink into the tide pools of your mind. It's weird and disturbing to see what's prowling around there, and you can't surface no matter how hard you try. Down you go, into the silences within yourself. Finally, you hit bottom and just hover there, weightless, face to face with those ancient fears and feral sensations that reach back to when man first slithered from the ooze, reared up on his hind legs and bolted for the nearest cave to steady up. It's very much like being insane, but far more intense because you're so aware of it. Mastering these feelings, the inner tension of being strung taut between fear and desire, is the fundamental challenge for the wall climber.

It is one thing to simply battle your way up a wall, jaw clenched, heart thumping like a paddle wheel. But to thrive up there, to dominate the climbing with confidence, to feel like you belong, requires a transformation of character hard to accept for a young climber. Up there with Ron on my first El Cap bivy, it seemed strangely unfair to have to grow all the way up at nineteen. I refused (in fact, passed out from weariness), then woke with a start at the emptiest hour of the night, completely disoriented. I writhed a bit, and came taut to the rope with a jerk. My shoulders and head flopped over the ledge and I might as well have been peering over the edge of the world. Mother of God!

Ron, sitting bolt upright beside me, said, "We're in trouble, big bloody trouble." Only then did I realize just how high we fools had flown. Then Ron started laughing and when I looked over at him, with his gravedigger's grin, I realized I wasn't looking at a young tough from Sheffield anymore. And all the tension we'd hauled up there suddenly vanished. I sat awake for a moment longer, voluptuous with fatigue, then fell back and slept the sleep of the dead.

By mid-morning the next day we were well into the upper corners, more than 2,500 feet up the wall and into the really prime terrain. And loving it despite the lines getting snagged, our feet aching from standing in slings, the grime and grit and aluminum oxide from the carabiners stinging our hands, the flesh barked and torn, shoulders aching from thirty-pound slings of nuts and fifty carabiners. Our throats were raw, teeth gummed, lips cracked, tongues like rawhide because you can never bring enough water, neck and arms flame red, backs crooked from hauling the bag, clothes spangled with tuna oil and sweat-soaked from sun to fry eggs by. But we didn't care because we were on El Capitan.

From the start, all the way up to the bivouac, I found myself measuring my reasons for confidence against the towering danger I was in, most of it imagined. But now I had gotten above all measuring, and my mind had taken a back seat to savor the chase as my body frantically went about its work. Nearing the top, the exposure is so enormous, and your perspective so distorted, that the horizontal world becomes incomprehensible. You're a granite astronaut, dangling in a kind of space/time warp, and the exhilaration is superb. Men talk of dreaming Gardens of Eden and cities of gold, but nothing can touch being pasted way up in the sky like that. It is a unique drama for which no tickets are sold.

Other routes are steeper, more exposed than the Nose. But no route has a more dramatic climax. The Harding headwall is short – 50 overhanging feet – and after a few friction steps, you're suddenly on level ground. But since Harding's day, some maniac had re-engineered the last belay so that it hung at the very brink of the headwall, where all 35 pitches spill down beneath your boots. It's a master stroke, that hanging belay, for it gives climbers a moment's pause at one of the most spectacular spots in all of American climbing. Cars creep along the valley's loop road three-quarters of a mile below, broad forests appear as brushed green carpets and, for one immortal moment, you feel like a giant in a world of ants. Then suddenly, it's over.

But it wasn't over. Ron had scrambled to the top, had hauled the bag and was yelling for me to hustle so we could get on with our lives. But I didn't move. I couldn't move. I kicked back in my stirrups and looked around. I didn't know why. I had never lingered before, always pressing on with gritted teeth, surging, fighting both myself and the climb to gain the top. Suddenly I was free of all that, of all the incessant rushing; so I just hung there and took it all in, and for the first time in my climbing career I seemed to fully appreciate what I was doing, how outrageous it was. Only by lingering did I get past all the sweat and vistas and paranoia and flashes of bliss, and only then did the whole disparate experience harmonize itself into a point of emotional symmetry and purpose.

The moment lasted about a minute. Without knowing it, I'd been chasing that moment since the first time I'd laced up climbing shoes. Yet even then, I couldn't really recognize the tune. (Some years later I was browsing through Bruce Chatwin's notes at the end of his book *Dreamtime,* and ran across the following paragraph: "A white explorer in Africa, anxious to press ahead with his journey, paid his porters for a series of forced marches. But they, almost within reach of their destination, set down their bundles and refused to budge. No amount of extra payment would convince them otherwise. They said they had to wait for their souls to catch up.")

Those first few moments on horizontal ground are so disorienting they hurl you into a transitional spin where little registers. A big wall is strong drink for a young mind. Few can handle it neat; most are hungover for hours, even days. Whether you've taken one day or one week, you are a different person than the one who started 3,000 feet below. I've heard of climbers hugging boulders, punching partners and weeping openly – some from relief, some sad that it was over. I've seen other climbers babbling incoherently, and I once saw a middle-aged Swiss team simply shake hands, abandon every stitch of their gear – ropes, rack, haulbags, the works – and stroll off for the trail down, their climbing careers made and finished right there. Ron and I only remember coiling ropes and bolting for the East Ledges descent route.

We got back down to the loop road about two that afternoon, exhausted by the nervous depression which always follows a wall. As we stumbled around a bend, El Capitan came into view, backlit and burning at the edges. For all the raw labor and anxieties of the climb, it was natural that, all the way up, I should wonder if I was committing more to a venture than it was actually worth, if I was putting too much into too little. But if there is anything of a magnitude that can blow a person off his feet, it's that first ground-level view of a wall he's just climbed. Too little? The second we saw it, Ron and I stood in the middle of the road and gaped up at it with our mouths open. It looked about ten miles high. And how long ago it seemed we'd been up there, and how strange, as though we'd seen it in a movie, or in a dream, and had suddenly woken up, half remembering what it was we dreamed.

There is so much in life one can thieve his way past, can wheedle over with guile and fancy talk, can ride out on the strength and toils of others. But not wall climbing. Nobody can climb so much as a single inch of one for you, so the victory is all yours.

Climbing a wall can be a monumental pain in the ass. No one could pay you enough to do it. A thousand dollars an hour would be too little, by far. But you wouldn't sell the least of the memories for ten times that sum. I remember dangling three thousand feet up the stupendous sodden wall of Angel Falls, where below and before us, rolling, mounting, sinking, rising, like huge swells in a huge green sea, the jungle fanned out to the edge of time. I remember hiking toward Carstenz Pyramid in Irian Jaya, where miles in the distance, outlined one against each other, the crests of a high cordillera seemed shuffled like a deck of stony cards – brusque peaks, bluish dips and notches, jutting arêtes swaying and falling in the harsh light, more inaccessible as we mounted on. And I remember peering over the lip of my hammock, lashed high on El Gran Trono Blanco, in Baja, Mexico, wondering how I was ever made alive. Few endeavors of man can touch a big wall for pure experience. Let's get into it.

CHAPTER 2

Grades and Ratings

In aid climbing (much more so than in free climbing), difficulty determines the techniques required. Rating that difficulty is a particularly useful introduction to the hows of it all.

A1 to A5

Determining how hard the climbing is and how long a team will take to complete the route is an inexact science. Everything changes except this: Whatever the rating, it is not as unequivocal as hard numbers (A1, A3+, and so on) might lead you to believe. Cracks get beaten out and placements become easier or harder as the number of ascents increases. The only certainty is that the route will change, as will the rating. The whole business of understanding ratings, and how they are arrived at, is crucial for a wall climber, so we'll look at both the decimal (difficulty rating) and grade (estimated time to make the ascent) ratings in a generic way, then study the nuances of the whole shebang.

Everyone has a little different understanding about what the grading system represents, but the journeyman's usage runs like this: An **A1** placement (the rating does not differentiate between a nut, a camming device, a piton, and so on) is normally easy to set, is rock solid, and is strong enough to sustain a good-sized fall. All anchoring matrixes are, or should be, built from A1 placements. When the leader, say, hammers in a peg, glances down to the belayer and chuckles, "A1, dude," that placement is bombproof. Period. There are grey areas here, however. The most common is "tricky" A1, meaning bombproof placements are obtainable, but you need experience and ingenuity to secure them. Still, 99 times out of 100, an A1 placement means a straightforward, secure piece of work.

A novel cam placement

Bill Hatcher photo

A2 placements can be creaky, perhaps decent pitons that must be tied off, or nuts, camming devices, and so on that are not in their optimal placement, and require some savvy and tinkering with to set. Still, A2 can generically be described as fairly solid, though not ideal placements, certainly good for body weight and probably adequate to arrest moderate falls.

A3 is where the going gets "real." This is advanced work – flaky, incipient cracks, micro pitons, hooks, copperheads, bashies (explained in detail later on)—the whole panoply of aid gimmicks, pushed close to their limits. Some wall climbers claim that as far as individual placements go, A3 is near the limit, that A4 and A5 are just more of the same. However, most veterans consider A3 to mean the placement is good enough for body weight, but little more. It will not arrest a fall. A3 is marginal going, at best.

A4 is shit-your-pants terrain, and is strictly for experts. An A4 placement is so marginal that it may pop when tested, and it only remains in place by the grace of God. An A4 placement can never hold a fall. Generally, A4 refers to a stretch of extremely dicey placements which would "zipper" en mass, shooting out like cloves from a holiday ham, should the leader ping.

Above every other definition, **A5** means danger. A5 always refers to a string of placements so marginal it takes not only God, but all the angels and saints to keep them in place. If one placement goes, they all go, and physical harm is almost assured. You may hit a ledge or swing into a corner. Only the most experienced aid climbers roll the dice on an A5 pitch.

GRADES

The decimal system tells us how difficult a climb is. The attending grade rating tells us how long an experienced climber will take to complete a given route.

Grade
I.   One to three hours.
II. Three to four hours.
III. Four to six hours. A strong half day.
IV. Full day. Emphasis on full.
V.   One to two days. Bivouac is usually unavoidable.
VI. Two or more days on the wall.

The decimal rating (A1-A5) is a relatively objective appraisal of difficulties, usually arrived at through consensus. The grade rating is posited as objective, but it uses the theoretical "experienced climber" as the example of how long a given route should take. Compare the grade rating with the par rating on a golf course. A par five means a honed golfer can usually hole the ball in five shots, rarely less, but a hacker will smile at a bogey six. Likewise, a world-class team in top form can almost always crank a grade V in one day, whereas the intermediate climber had best come prepared to spend the night.

Since Jim Madson and Kim Schmitz made a two-bivouac ascent of the Dihedral Wall on El Capitan (in 1965), and Jeff Foote and Steve Roper flashed the regular route on Half Dome in the same year, speed climbing walls has become

---

fashionable. The art was pushed to its logical conclusion with the first one-day ascent of the Nose, on El Capitan, in 1975, an exercise that has become obligatory for hardmen (who continually strive to shave minutes off the fastest time). While such efforts are not unreasonable goals for serious athletes, few teams are prepared to do so, and speed climbing should not be construed as a required goal for wall climbers.

Such is the rating system in broad strokes. Now let's look at the nuances.

If a climb is rated Grade VI, 5.10, A4, what can we know for sure by reading such a rating? The grade VI tells us that if we're going about our business in a normal way (not trying to speed climb), we can expect to spend at least two days on the wall. The grade rating cannot tell us exactly how long we will take, because the rating cannot take into account the vagaries of weather, the length of the days (which change considerably from spring to summer to fall, etc....), nor the relative efficiency of a given team. The 5.10 rating is much more objective, so no matter the season or the team, you'd better be able to free climb at a 5.10 level, or you will most likely have to retreat. The same goes for the A4 rating. Though aid ratings routinely change, if a route carries an A4 rating, it is far saner to assume that you will find very difficult aid climbing, rather than to hope the placements have gotten easier since the route was last rated. Now let's look at what the ratings cannot tell us.

A grade VI, 5.10, A4 rating can apply equally to an eight-pitch, three-day route with merely one pitch of A4 and a short, well-protected section of 5.10, as well as to a horrendous, thirty-pitch, ten-day nailup, with multiple horror-show A4 pitches, and bold, runout 5.10 face climbing on burnished warts above tied-off blades. Because most guide books are topo-style guides, eschewing written descriptions, the subjective perils of a given route are rarely stated. The climber is not kept in the dark, however, because the general difficulty of a route usually becomes evident when it's in plain sight, and the intimidation which one feels when looking up at a massive chunk of stone roughly corresponds to the effort and skill required to climb it. The other indicator is public opinion. If a route is a widowmaker, it will certainly have a reputation. And if the route has been climbed too few times to have a reputation, common sense will keep you from trying it unless you are up for the task.

NUANCES IN THE DECIMAL RATING

The previous, generic summary of the decimal system was the generally accepted structure up to perhaps 1980. Since then, aid specialists have pushed the standards even farther out, resulting in a "new wave" treatment of the rating system, including new terminology, fresh appraisals, and different attitudes. The gist of the new wave canon runs like this:

A0 Also known as "french-free," involves using gear to make progress, but generally no aiders are required (stepping/ hanging on protection, pulling up on nuts, etc.) Examples: Half Dome regular route; sections of the Nose route on El Cap; the first two pitches of the El Cap's West Face (either a quick 5.10, A0 with three points of aid, or tricky 5.11c).

A1 Easy aid. Placements straightforward and solid. No risk of any piece pulling out. Aiders generally required. Fast and simple for clean aid, although clean placements usually take more time and savvy. Examples: (clean) the non-5.12 version of the Salathé headwall; Prodigal Son on Angel's Landing; Touchstone Wall in Zion.

A2 Moderate aid. Placements generally solid but possibly awkward and strenuous to place. Maybe a tenuous placement or two above good pro with no fall danger. Examples: the Right side of El Cap Tower (nailing); Moonlight Buttress and Space Shot in Zion (clean).

A2+ Like A2, but usually several tenuous placements above good pro. 20- to 30-foot fall potential but with little danger of hitting anything. Route-finding abilities may be required. Examples: The new wave grades of Mescalito and the Shield on El Cap; the Kor route on the Titan in the Fisher Towers area.

A3: Hard aid. Testing methods required. Involves many tenuous placements in a row. Generally solid placements (which could hold a fall) found within a pitch. Long fall potential, up to 50 feet (6 to 8 placements ripping), but generally safe from serious peril. Several hours required to complete a pitch, due to the complexity of placements. Examples: The Pacific Ocean Wall, lower crux pitches (30 feet between original bolts on many fixed copperheads); Standing Rock in the desert (the crux being a traverse on the first pitch with very marginal gear with 30-foot swing potential into a corner).

A3+ Like A3, but with dangerous fall potential. Tenuous placements (like marginal tied-off pins, or a hook on a fractured edge) after long stretches of body-weight pieces (here body-weight placements are considered, for all practical purposes, any piece of gear not solid enough to hold a fall). Potential to get hurt if good judgment is not exercised. Time required to lead an A3+ pitch generally exceeds 3 hours for experienced aid climbers. Example: Pitch 3 of "Days of No Future" on Angel's Landing in Zion, the crux being 50 feet of birdbeaks and tied-off blades in soft sandstone, followed by a blind, marginal Friend placement in loose rock which was hard to test properly, all this above a ledge.

A4 Serious aid. Lots of jeopardy. 60- to 100-foot fall potentials common, with uncertain landings far below. Examples: pitches on the Kaliyuga on Half Dome, the Radiator on Abraham, Zion. The Giraffe on El Gran Trono Blanco, Mexico.

A4+ More serious than A4. Leads generally take many hours to complete, requiring the climber to suffer long periods of uncertainty and fear. Often requires ballet-like efficiency of movement in order not to upset the tenuous integrity of marginal placements. Examples: the "Welcome to Wyoming" pitch (formerly the "Psycho Killer" pitch) on the Wyoming Sheep Ranch on El Cap, requiring 50 feet of climbing through a loose, broken and rotten Diorite roof with very marginal, scary placements – like stoppers wedged in between two loose, shifting, rope-slicing slivers of rock, all this over a big jagged ledge which would surely break bones. The pitch is then followed by a hundred feet of hooking, interspersed with a few rivets to the belay.

A5 Extreme aid. Nothing really trustworthy of catching a fall for the entire pitch. A5 rating reserved for pitches with no bolts or rivets (holes).

A6 (Theoretical Grade) A5 climbing with marginal belays which will not hold a fall. The leader pings, and it's into the beyond for the whole team.

A characteristic of adventure is that inherent difficulties cannot be precisely defined, let alone rated. Grades of A4 or harder may impress the masses, but anyone in the know will tell you that, owing to the incredible diversity of difficulties involved with wall climbing (especially the hard routes), ultra-specific wall grades are only an indicator. Most A5 leads have dangerous fall potential early in the pitch (with the danger of hitting a slab or ledge), and the battle usually continues up on marginal pieces – many barely body weight, and none very secure – for most of the way. A5 pitches are given the A5 grade because they are top difficulty on an arbitrary scale. Beyond this, a precise distinction is illusory.

Historically, the A5 grade has always been the most difficult thing going. What they called A5 on the original North American Wall ascent, for example, would be considered A2 or A3 by new-wave standards; likewise, A5 on the original Pacific Ocean Wall route would be considered relatively tame (A3+: a reasonably safe, 60- to 80-foot fall) by today's standards. The grey area here is the fact that these two routes have become far easier with repeated ascents and better technology. Presently, new-wave A5 means a dangerous or death fall potential on marginal body weight placements. Cutting-edge aid climbing just gets bolder with time, yet to let the scale get out of control with grades of A6 and up simply renders the grade system useless.

Conclusion: it's sketchy to put a number on something so massive and diverse as a big wall, but we stick with the basic A1 to A5 system for describing individual pitches – with A1 indicating safe passage and A5 meaning extreme danger – understanding the numbers are an indicator of difficulties: a value judgment.

There is a long steep road between where you are now sitting and the top of Trango Tower, and the journey starts with a single placement.

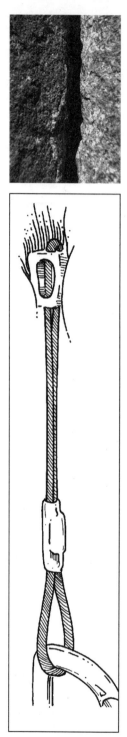

Even the most difficult aid climbs use much the same gear as that used on traditional free climbs, so we start with clean protection, understanding that the guidelines and expectations are slightly different when the standard gear is used for aid.

Your first few aid climbs, and indeed your initial wall ascents, will be (or should be) on the same routes where countless other aspiring wall aces learned the basics. Remember: minimum impact is the rule. Look at "Serenity Crack" in Yosemite Valley to see the destructiveness of runaway pitoning. If we want the standard practice aid climbs to last, and the trade walls as well, we've got to be conscientious about preserving them. That means clean climbing whenever possible.

I'm ashamed to admit it, but early on in my (J. L.) climbing career I almost singlehandedly destroyed The Prow, a short, steep aid route on Washington Column. The route had been climbed perhaps six or eight times, and the placements were getting a little loose from repeated pitoning and cleaning. Rather than cock around with weird nut configurations or in-between-sized piton placements, I hammered in the next size up, and by main force, reduced a borderline A4 pitch to A2 – and ruined the rock in the process. Not the way to go.

Even rudimentary aid climbing assumes a sound understanding of basic gear and standard placements. Because basic aid placements do not differ from those used on free climbing routes, the first few times you go aid climbing the emphasis is not on seeing how poor a placement you can get away with; rather, try to get accustomed with the whole business of standing in aid slings, building a ladder of placements, and the other things we'll discuss shortly. The fundamental procedures must become automatic (and quickly are) long before you go out and start tackling climbs where every last placement is a crap shoot. So your first few aid climbs should be easy ones. They'll most likely require only clean climbing gear.

When an aid climb can be done completely without pitons, climbers will sometimes change the "A" in the rating to "C" – for clean. (A1 becomes C1, A2 becomes C2, and so on.)

Individual Aid Placements

Clean tools, such as camming units, tapers, and natural anchors, offer the mainstay placements for the majority of standard aid routes (most easy to moderate aid climbs go completely clean). Placing a nut is easier and faster than placing a piton. And with the advent of Friends and other camming devices (spring-loaded camming devices, or SLCDs), the aid climber's task has been further simplified. Compare reaching up and inserting a bomber #2 Friend with grappling around with both hands to slam in a big heavy angle piton. You'll get to the pitons soon enough, and it's better to have the procedures down pat before you do.

Aid placements can be, and often are, more marginal than those required for free climbing. Examples include the placement of a friend where only two cams are in contact with the rock, or a micro taper in a shallow seam. So long as the piece can hold body weight in the direction of pull, it's a viable aid placement. One prefers the most bomber piece possible, granted, but often due to terrain, time considerations, and so on, a marginal piece may have to do.

This is not the venue for a review of what constitutes a good or bad nut or SLCD. For that information, refer to *Climbing Anchors*. However, you do want to learn just how much, or how little, a piece of gear can hold, and the sanest way to experiment is to do so where you can't possibly get hurt. The solution is easy. Build a rack of tapers, micros, SLCDs, and so on, grab a pair of slings, go to a section of rock that has a series of cracks right off the ground, and

Clean gear: (from left) Black Diamond Camalot, cabled Friend, Wired Bliss TCU, RP brass taper, Lowe Ball-nut.

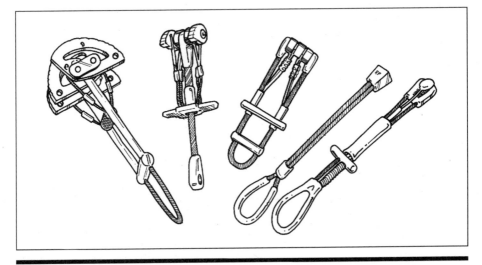

experiment. Try every kind of placement imaginable. Clip the slings into them and weight them with your body. Jump up and down on them and learn just what will work and what won't. Keep the placements very low, so your feet are mere inches above the ground. And keep your legs straight so you land on your feet. Be prepared for the borderline placements to pop if you shock-load them. Be careful about dusting your ankles when they do.

To learn is to experiment, to keep trying the problematic or improbable placement. You'll never realize what will and will not hold until you push the gear to its limit. Develop an eye for the ideal placement, and try to make it straightaway. A couple of sessions can be very fruitful. And always, when you're learning the fine points, do it at ground level.

PITONS

When a suitable berth for clean pro cannot be found, it's time for the pitons, aka "pegs," or "pins." Placing a piton involves picking the right size, placing it in a crack, and hammering on it. Pitons scar the rock, and are time-consuming to place and remove. But the advancements in

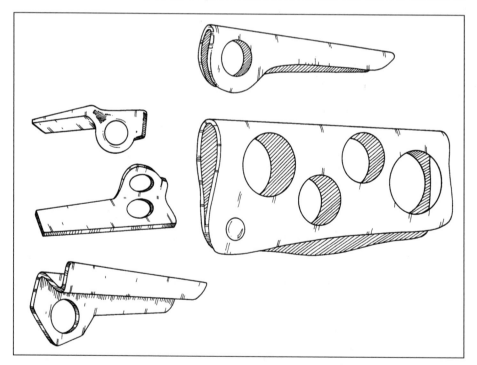

Pitons (clockwise from upper right):
1-inch angle, 2-inch bong, Leeper Z-ton, Bugaboo, Lost Arrow

mechanical gear haven't completely eliminated the necessity of pitons for some vertical adventures, and so far as certain placements go – particularly thin, incipient seams – it seems doubtful if anything but pitons will ever do. Difficult "nailing" requires pitons, period. Since shallow seams or thin, bottoming cracks are often impossible without pegs, the smaller varieties are most often used. Bigger pegs (¾" to bongs) have been largely replaced by nuts and SLCDs, save for the oddball placement (such as a weird-shaped pocket or an extreme flare, where camming devices wouldn't work). Perhaps someday a more complete assortment of tools will enable all but the most incipient cracks to be climbed without pins. For now, pitoncraft is still required for anything but easy to moderate walls.

The only American company making pitons on any significant scale – as they have for decades – is Black Diamond (née Chouinard). There are four basic designs. Knifeblades (called Bugaboos in the larger sizes) come in six sizes, from ⅛ to ³⁄₁₆ inch in width, and from 3 to 4⅞ inches in length. Precision grinding ensures a constant taper. Lost Arrows (aka horizontals) come in eight sizes, from ⁵⁄₃₂ to ⁹⁄₃₂ inch in width, and from 1¾ to 4⅝ inches long. Angles come in six sizes, from ½ to 1½ inches in width. Bongs are big angles, from 2 to 4 inches in width. The RURP (Realized Ultimate Reality Piton), a postage stamp-sized peg with a thin, half-inch long blade, is for aid only.

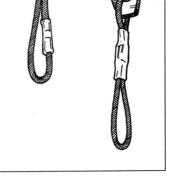

The designs have changed little in 20 years. The hot-forging method is age-old and unsurpassed, and the 4130 chrome-moly steel is harder than granite. European imports generally are inferior. All told, Black Diamond pitons are probably the finest mass-produced line in the world.

A5 Birdbeak, and the Black Diamond RURP

A typical starter piton rack will include several knifeblades, a half dozen arrows, two to three each of the "Baby Angles" (½-inch and ⅝-inch angles), and one each of the larger angles (¾-, 1-, 1¼-, and 1½-inch). Generally, it is nice to have some "sawed off" pitons in the larger sizes, for pockets and pin scars (discussed later).

Other pitons include the A5 Birdbeak, a thin hooking type piton, also known as a "seam hook," particularly useful for hooking in seams. The Leeper Z-ton, a specialty piton, is used independently or stacked with an angle piton. Occasionally on old classic routes you find a fixed soft iron piton with a welded ring for the clip-in. These are relics, and are not to be trusted. Titanium pegs have been coming out of the old Soviet bloc for nearly a decade, but they are exceedingly rare, and are only durable enough for a placement or two.

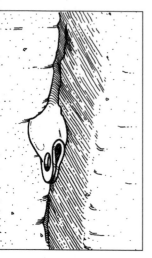

General Considerations

Pitoncraft is fast becoming a lost art. Many trade routes in Yosemite (like the Zodiac and the Shield on El Capitan) are sad reminders of this, and are rapidly being demolished by frenzied hammers. The dilemma is that the subtle points of pounding iron, though simple in principle, can only be learned through experience, so the destruction of routes remains a necessary evil. The more ascents, the more the cracks degenerate no matter how gently the hammer is wielded. Just bear in mind that efficient pitoning is something different than setting railroad ties. An expert nailer will often place a solid piece with a few deft hammer blows.

Quickly finding the optimum placement requires a good eye, which comes from experience. Don't overdrive the pin, which leads to a difficult pin to clean (clean means to remove) and avoidable destruction to the stone. At first, the hammer will feel awkward in your hand, and you'll probably overdrive most pins. In time, you'll get more confidence, and will know when enough is enough. Cleaning your own leads is a good lesson (more on this later on). Beware of that "one last hit" which transforms a "bomber" piton to one that's "fixed" (fixed means unclean-able). Also, beware of placements in hard to remove spots, such as directly under a small roof, where a pin may go in easy, but for lack of space to swing the hammer in any direction but directly into your eye, you cannot clean it. Again, many routes are ruined by the heavy hammer, so bear in mind that good pitoncraft entails more finesse than force.

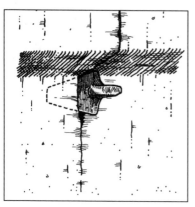

Poor placements of pitons may make them impossible to remove

Hammertime

A hefty hammer is the tool for big wall nailing. A good hammer is well-balanced, has a nice square head (for nailing in corners), a hole in the head for clipping a carabiner into (for cleaning purposes), and a pick designed for both cleaning pitons and placing mashheads. Many hammers made specifically for big wall climbing have been manufactured in the past, including the original Chouinard Yosemite hammer, the Forrest big wall hammer, and the A5 hammer. None of these are currently available. If you ever get a chance to buy one, do so. These are not only collector's items, but the best tools as well.

The Black Diamond big wall hammer is the finest one currently available. It's a well-built article that will last many walls. European imports are also available, but are generally too light for heavy-duty wall use. In a pinch, a modified geology hammer or even a 22-ounce framing hammer can work (but not that well).

The hammer should be connected to the climber with a cord/shoulder sling system, the length of which must allow full arm's reach. The cord which connects the hammer to the climber should be long enough so the hammer hangs below the feet when not in use. This prevents "tripping" on the hammer as one climbs upward. For versatility, a hammer holster (on the waist) allows the hammer to be tucked out of the way – important for mixed free/aid pitches. A soft holster is desired over a hard, plastic one, which can chafe a climber's side like a burr under the saddle.

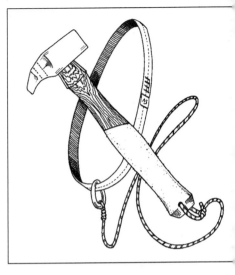

A5 hammer and sling

Placing Pitons

Just as we did with clean climbing devices, we first practice placing pitons at ground level. Clip in aid slings, or a few slings looped together, weight the placements and see how good or bad they are. Note: we do not practice driving pegs at a popular or even unpopular section of a sport crag any more than we take a can of spray paint to the Sistine Chapel to "experiment." Go to some scrappy part of a worthless cliff and experiment there. Anywhere there's rock, there will be rock that nobody wants to climb, and usually plenty of it. All you need are some cracks. Find an area far away from the crowd and slug it out.

Rock conditions are consistently variable, but normally, a piton should slide in about one third to halfway before hammering, and should go all the way to the eye when driven "home." First, eyeball the crack, then select a suitable pin. Place it in the most appropriate spot (only experience can tell you exactly where that will be, but try to find that section of crack that best corresponds with the symmetry of the pin, where the pin is "keyed in"). Holding it in the fingers of one hand, lightly set it with a couple of hammer blows. Miss the pin, smack your fingers; but if you don't keep ahold of it before setting, you're certain to drop a lot of pins. So set it with a few light taps.

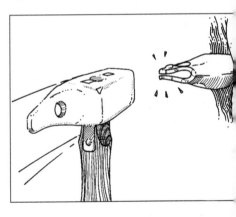

Driving an angle piton in with deft blows

Ideally, the pin will have a clear and rising ringing sound as you drive it home, like a scale on a glockenspiel. A dull thunking sound usually means poor rock or a marginal placement, where little surface area of the pin is contacting the stone. You will probably not get the perfect placement right off, and might have to try several different pegs to get the best one; but you'll quickly learn to grab the appropriate one at a glance. Basic pitoning is for the most part self-evident – or becomes so after a few hours.

Each different kind of pin works best in a particular kind of placement. And there are little nuances about placing them that you can only discover by placing them. For

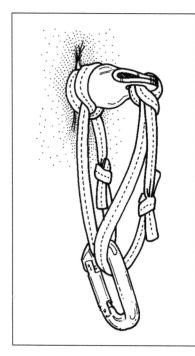

instance, you can only hit a knifeblade so hard before it will buckle; a Lost Arrow won't ring much unless the rock is diamond hard; a larger-angle pin's placement is often marginal unless much of the spine and the two running edges are contacting the rock, and so on. As mentioned, key things about the relative security of various placements is learned by removing them. You'll quickly understand what works for a given placement, and most importantly, why. You're not going to get ideal, bombproof pegs the first couple of times. There is art required here. So don't go slamming the pegs like a blacksmith, trying to force a solid piece. You'll only maul the pin and trash the rock.

We could spend pages here discussing the minutia, and never learn what you can in a couple hours of making placements. So find that section of junk cliff and tap away. Learn how to wield the hammer, how soft to swing it, how to keep your fingers clear once the peg is set, how to quickly spot the placements, and all the rest. (Cleaning will be discussed shortly.)

An angle piton tied off short with a sling, and safeguarded against loss with a longer keeper sling tied through the eye.

Reducing Leverage with Tie-off Slings

Tie-off slings, 27- to 30-inch lengths of ½- or ⁹⁄₁₆-inch tubular webbing, are tied with a water knot. These are used only to tie off pitons to reduce leverage. The greater tensile strength of beefier webbing is sacrificed for the tight cinching ability of the thinner article.

Tie-offs reduce the leverage on pitons which "bottom out." An overhand knot can be used to tie pitons off, but a clove hitch is quicker and easier to untie afterwards. A longer

Pitons not driven to the eye must be tied off short with a sling: on the left, with a girth hitch, or on the right, a slip knot.

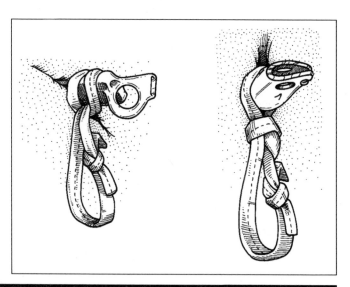

"keeper sling" tie-off, looped through the eye and clipped in, will prevent losing the pin if it pulls out. (Make sure the load is not on the keeper sling.)

Stacking

If the placement is a shallow pocket, say, and the exact piton size isn't available, one must "stack" two or more pitons in the same placement for a secure piece). Since stacked pins are often marginal, meaning they can fall out when you're arranging them, the first consideration is that you don't drop the lot. A hero loop threaded through the eyes of stacked pins secures them.

The concept behind stacked (or "nested") pins is a simple one: shimming one loose piton with others to get a tight, composite placement. Imagine a hole drilled into the top of an anvil. You need to anchor off to the hole, but don't have anything that precisely fits it. You only have a handful of nails. So you place the nail that best fills the hole, then start shimming it with others until, owing to the outward pressure and the combined surface area of the nails, the whole works might hold. This is essentially the concept: a hole or section of crack won't accept any piton on your rack – or at least not to your satisfaction. You're left to try to construct a composite placement, trying to fill up the hole or crack by increasing the tension within it and getting the various edges of the pins to bite. Nested pins are most often required in shallow, rounded, or beaten-out placements. Not all stacks are dicey; some are A1. And after you get a knack for it, sketchy placements can be made considerably better if you know a few tricks.

The standard combinations are: stacking two angles together; extending the breadth of a small angle by driving a Lost Arrow or Bugaboo along its running edges; stacking a series of knifeblades and/or arrows; and stacking angles with Leeper Z-tons.

As a rule, stacked pins are used in two basic instances. On popular aid climbs, the cracks inevitably get beaten-out. Since this happens incrementally, at some time the crack's width will be a little too big or too small for the standard pins. Trying to bash an oversized pin into an undersized crack is a fool's pursuit. As mentioned, simply shore up the loose peg by nesting a thin pin along its running edges. Also common is a large shallow hole, such as found on Yosemite's Serenity Crack. Clean gear can sometimes be used here, but often two large angles must be stacked for large shallow holes. For

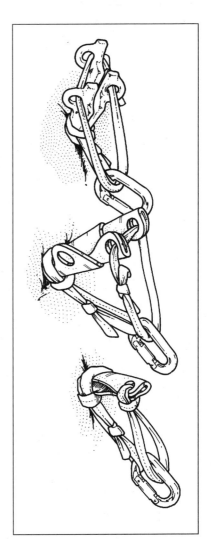

Various pitons stacked and tied off. They all have keeper slings to prevent their loss should they pull out.

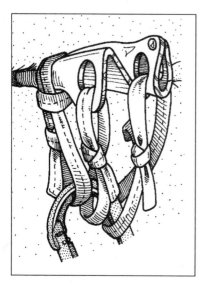

Stacked and tied-off
Leeper Z-ton with a one-
inch angle. Keeper slings
guard the stack from loss.

off-sized piton holes ("pin scars"), especially bottomed and beaten-out ones, a sawed-off piton can often take the place of stacked pins. A set of sawed-off pegs in the larger sizes (¾-inch and up), shortened to about 3½ inches total length, are useful for many routes, especially the much-traveled trade routes.

The second mode concerns the weird-sized (usually bottoming) flare or pod, where you have to nest unusual and often creative combinations of pins to try to fill the hole – like the nails in the anvil. The only way to discover what does and does not work is, again, to experiment. Creativity is key. There are no rules, though the standard combinations just mentioned are usually good starting points. Any blend that works is the solution. The more surface area you can get contacting the rock, the more secure the placement usually is. That means that adding pins to the outside of the stacked grouping is commonly, but not always, the answer.

Expanding flakes were once the nailer's nightmare. But clever use of nuts and camming units have reduced "expando" nailing from its voodoo reputation to a fairly sane activity (for the most part). In years past, before even chockstones were available, you can imagine the horror of pitoning your way up a flake as thin as a flapjack. Each additional placement would expand the flake, so that the harder you drove in the next piece, the looser became the pin you were standing on. This was nerve-wracking work, and climbs like the "Flake" pitch on the West Face of Sentinel were grim affairs.

If the expanding crack accepts camming units, the climbing is generally safe and easy. However, the cruxes of many modern nail-ups are still thin, expanding flakes, where a "feel" for the placement is necessary. More on thin expanding nailing later on.

Removing or "Cleaning" Pitons

A good nailer is an aggressive cleaner, but is aware of rock destruction. Knocking a pin back and forth the full length it can travel is the most efficient method. Tap it till it's loose, then pluck it out with your hands. Experience will show you when a pin is loose enough to remove by hand. To prevent dropping a pin, a "cleaning biner" attached to a sling is clipped in as the pin gets loose (large Bonaiti D's, taped onto a cleaning sling or cable are the best rigs); pulling and applying leverage with the cleaner biner/sling aids in final removal. Prying with the pick of the hammer through the eye of the pin will often help. But be careful; the pin can shoot out when least expected. Remember to keep your hands well clear for power strokes, and strive to know when a pin is working loose enough for hand removal – or expect to drop a lot of pins.

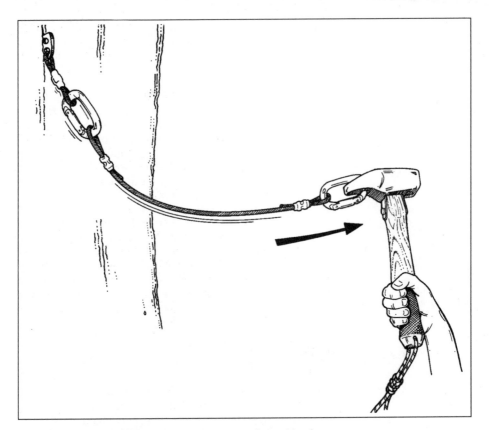

The funkness device in action.

For serious nailing routes, get or make a "funkness device," a two-foot swaged cable (⅜₂-inch) with loops on both ends. In addition to cleaning pins, they are ideal for removing copperheads, birdbeaks, and stuck tapers. Swing the hammer out and yank the placement from the rock. Hammers with a carabiner hole in the head allow for easy attachment to the funkness device; otherwise, a hero loop around the top of the handle – below the head – makes for a passable attachment point. Pitons in expanding flakes often require a funkness device for final removal.

Another point in cleaning etiquette: hammer pitons back and forth predominately upward, above the horizontal. Known as "constructive scarring," this creates nut placements over time. Most important on soft rock.

Other Basic Piton Placements

Possibilities are often many for a given section of rock; an eye for placements and good judgment are keys in choosing the most secure and efficient placement. Other crafty placements include stacking camming devices with blocks of wood (for wide cracks), clean uses of a piton placed in a hole (as found on the Shield route on El Cap), a clean stack of a piton and a stopper, a bong placed sideways, or a thin brass nut placed in the bottom of a pin scar. Often, the more ingenuity involved in creating a solid placement, the better. The main considerations consist of efficiently finding the best placement while factoring in the ease of removal.

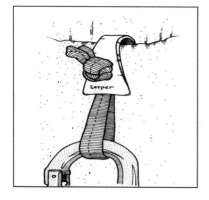

Basic hook placement on a good shelf

Hook Placements

Some easy and moderate aid routes require the use of a hook or two, so the basic "Chouinard Hook" should be tested on small shelves and nubbins near the ground before hooking on the high crag. Remember that when a hook "pops," it comes off hard. How hard? There's the story of a woman who scaled the Direct Route on Half Dome. She set a hook, stepped high in her aid sling and jumped onto it. The hook popped, caught on the front of her shirt, and as her leg straightened, she essentially stripped her top half right down to her birthday suit, in which she finished the route. Surely this story has been romanced, but the point is: when testing dicey placements, keep your face clear lest they pop. More on hooking in the advanced topics.

FIXED GEAR

Fixed gear is common on popular aid routes. Always test it thoroughly. When you don't, bad things can happen. Take the notorious "Groove" pitch on the Shield, El Capitan. The pitch ascends a 90-foot incipient fissure in which most of the gear is fixed (from ascents since the late '70s). Most placements are RURPS and copperheads, too buried to clean, though countless parties have tried – further thrashing the gear. For a dozen years the Groove was almost entirely fixed. Finally, when I (J. M.) soloed it in 1984, I didn't need to place a single piece of gear in the Groove. As successive parties climbed the route, the horror stories grew about the Groove pitch – of copperheads hanging by a single strand of an already thin cable, and RURP slings bleached white from UV rays and horribly frayed from hammers. Troy Johnson was near the end of the pitch, jumped onto a copperhead without testing it, and shot off the overhanging wall for a hundred and twenty footer, zippering the entire pitch. Test everything. Always. And back it up if you have any doubts.

Copperheads fixed in a flare (left), and in a slot (right).

RIVET HANGERS

On the big routes, shallow drilled holes are filled with various sorts of rivets (dowels, Z-macs, or best, machine head bolts) that must be clipped for progress. Rivets are like bolts, in that they are drilled holes filled with metal. Unlike bolts, however, rivets are only designed to hold body weight. Specially swaged cable loops called rivet hangers are used to connect to rivets, though wired tapers with the taper pushed down will do in a pinch. Rivet hangers with ³⁄₃₂-inch cable (with strength of 950 pounds) are most commonly used, but sometimes the rivet is nearly flush with the rock, requiring a thinner cable rivet hanger. For machine head rivets, the Australian RP hangers are preferred. Also available are "key-

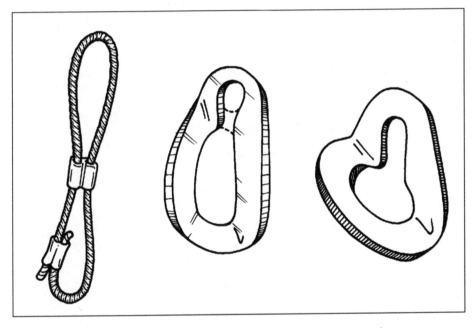

hole hangers," that are essential for hangerless bolts that you can count on finding here and there. No? Dig it: I (J.L.) gained a sling belay about a mile up El Capitan and found two bolts. One had a hanger but was hanging about halfway out of the wall. The second had no hanger and the rivet head was virtually flush to the wall. A keyhole hanger would have worked, and I didn't have one. Since the next pitch started out with RURPS, I was forced to belay and haul from the one bunk bolt. By the time my partner finally got to a bolt after about fifty feet of dicey aid on the following pitch, I felt like Father Time's older brother.

Rivet hangers: (from left) Cabled swaged unit, and keyhole hanger.

THE SYSTEM: A Look Ahead

The riddle about trying to explain the process of climbing big walls is that often we must put the cart before the horse. The most straightforward way is what we're doing – studying the components and procedures of the aid climbing system, learning a little more about the whole as we move through the parts. If at times we get a little ahead of ourselves, we'll only be slightly ahead, and the big picture will come into focus soon enough. There is little sense in discussing general concerns about your first aid lead before we familiarize ourselves with the particulars.

Understand that the basic system is very simple: you build a ladder of gear up the side of a rock wall, clipping the rope through the successive placements (for protection), and gaining altitude by climbing up the steps of your aid slings. The many tricks and specialized gear are useful in that they make the system safer and the mode of ascent more efficient. While it may seem confusing to read, the general principles virtually describe themselves once you get out onto the lead. There are numerous ways to do any one of the various procedures, but for the most basic things, there is really only one way to do them, and it becomes self-evident after only a few leads. Experience will help you understand the system thoroughly and quickly, and future experiments will just be exercises in refining your technique.

Aid Slings and Weighting Placements

When the placement is made, it's time to get on it. For each successive placement, the aim is to get as high as you comfortably can, enabling you to reach above to make the next placement. The higher you are, the more rock you have to choose from to secure the appropriate piece, as well as keeping the pieces spaced reasonably far apart. If the pieces are too closely spaced, a 150-foot lead can devour more gear than you can carry, as well as taking too much time. More than anything, an ace aid climber is an efficient one.

Modern aid slings (aka "etriers," "aiders," or "stirrups") are fashioned from sewn webbing, featuring four, five, or even six steps. Most commonly used are four- and five-step aiders, with sub-second and sub-top steps. Knotted aiders can be crafted from a long piece of 1-inch tubular webbing, but are inferior to sewn aiders. Sewn steps are far easier to place a foot into. Also, if you climb a number of walls in a few short months, the knots in hand-tied aid slings can result in grievous corns and bunions on the sides of your feet, for the boot is continually rubbing up against the knot.

The best all-around aiders are sewn, rigid-step, four-and five-step articles. Especially when it's windy and the aiders spend half the time whipping around your head, it's nice to have a stiff opening to throw your foot into.

For long and difficult routes, you'll want to rig your aiders with "grab loops," consisting of short loops of supertape webbing on the top of each aider. This saves your hands, as you are continually pulling yourself up by the grab loop (the alternative is to grab the carabiner).

When purchasing sewn aiders, buy them from the same manufacturer. Hold them up against one another and compare. The dimensions of the steps (step length) should be precisely the same for both aiders, because you'll want to have both feet at the same level while standing in them.

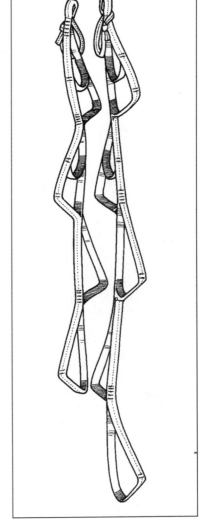

Basic pair of aiders with a top grab loop and sub-second and sub-top steps.

Once an individual placement is made, the climber 1) clips the piece off with a biner; 2) clips in the aider; 3) steps into a lower rung. Because you don't want to add distance to a fall if the placement should fail, you usually don't clip the lead rope into the piece until your waist is even with it – as you're stepping up in the slings. Continue climbing up the rungs until you're high enough to place the next piece. You normally climb no higher than the second step, or sub-second step.

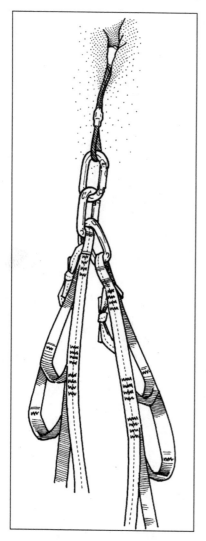

Two-aider method. Note: the first aider biner can also be clipped directly to the placement for three inches of extra reach.

"Top-stepping," when the feet are in the top step or sub-top step, is performed on lower-angle terrain (80 degrees or less), and occasionally on the steeper stuff (when no available placement is reachable from the second step). Continuous top-stepping on steep rock is almost always more strenuous and time consuming than simply to make placements from the second step. On overhanging turf, top-stepping is downright impossible because, since your upper body is teetering back beyond the vertical, gravity is always pushing you off.

AIDER METHODS

For climbs with short aid sections, the two-aider method is preferred. Although it's possible to stand with only one foot in one aider, it's easier to have both feet placed at the same level, each in separate aiders, especially while standing in the higher steps.

With two aiders (each aider having its own carabiner), one aider is clipped into the high piece; the climber transfers his weight onto it, unclips the lower aider from the lower piece, and clips it into the higher piece before climbing higher in the aider now clipped into the top piece. Both aider biners can be clipped directly into the placement biner(s), but it's usually best to clip the second aider into the top aider biner instead of clipping directly into the placement biner. This makes it easier to unclip the second aider once the next placement is secured (the weight must be on the initial, higher aider to do this). Sounds involved, but it's plain as water once you try it.

Though useful for short aid sections, the two-aider technique invites the dreaded "biner shift." This occurs when both aiders are clipped into the placement biner. When the weight is shifted from one aider to the other, the newly-weighted biner can shift suddenly to the lowest position on the placement biner (displacing the other aider biner), creating a sharp and sudden jolt which is often mistaken for the piece ripping out.

The sound can foul a rookie's knickers in a heartbeat.

Again: you're standing in your two aid slings, which are clipped, say, to a bomber hex. From the second steps, you reach up and slot a faithful taper. You clip a biner into said taper, reach down, unclip one aider from the hex, reach up and clip it into the taper, and shift your weight onto it. Next, you reach down and unclip the other aider, and instead of clipping off to the biner connected directly to the taper, you clip the aider into the biner on the other aid sling. When you repeat the process, you don't have to struggle trying to unclip from a weighted and cramped carabiner; you simply unweight from the lower aid sling, and unclip it. The disadvantage with this system is that the rungs of each aider are always at slightly different levels; but because you only use the two-aider technique when minimal aid is required, the inconvenience is a short one.

For walls with moderate amounts of aid, the three-aider method is usually favored. With three aiders, only two are used at any given time. The third, normally clipped onto a gear sling, is always poised to be the first aider clipped into the next placement. With the two-aider system, you often have your foot weighted in the very aider you want to unclip, and then clip off to the higher piece. Also, because the there are great tensions on the weighted piece, unclipping an aid sling can be a polecat – unless, as described, it is the last one on the chain, which you can unweight and then unclip. The three-aider technique eliminates these problems.

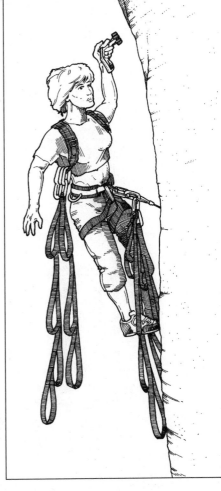

Remember, after the third (or "free") aider is placed on the higher piece, one of the two lower aiders is also clipped into the high piece while the other is clipped off to your rack. It becomes the free aider, and is ready to be leapfrogged (clipped first) onto the next higher placement.

For serious aid, the four-aider method is the ticket, and is almost always used. Two matched aiders are clipped into a single biner. That gives you two sets of two aiders, each on single biners. Accordingly, each aider set is leapfrogged from a placement, to the rack, then to the new placement.

Again: after one pair is clipped into the higher piece, the lower pair is clipped off to the side (on the rack, or wherever), ready to be used on the next higher placement. The best system uses one four-step and one five-step aider on each biner, since it is rare to need both feet in the fifth step. It is very important that each pair has the same length steps so that the feet are level while making the next placement.

Four-aider method.

Note: take care when levering a piece as shown in this illustration.

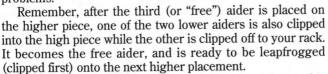

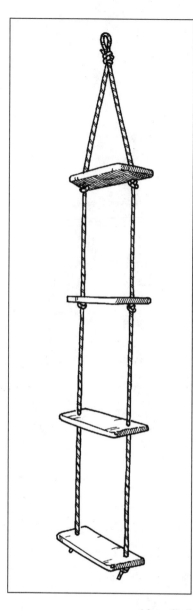

European aid ladders

These descriptions are confounding if you can't picture what is happening – which is hard to do with unfamiliar gear and techniques. A good way to grasp the whole McGilla is to read through the written descriptions a few times, go out and flounder for a few hours, then come back and read the descriptions again. Better yet, go out to the garage and work through the whole process with your aiders and a couple of nails or hooks (or whatever works) attached to the wall. However tedious these descriptions are, you need to know them thoroughly. Take consolation that, even if you need to work through them word by word, you'll only have to do so once, because the whole business is obvious once you do it.

OTHER AIDER SYSTEMS

Other aider systems include European and Russian. Europeans generally use aiders which resemble a ladder: stiff (often wooden) steps are joined on either side by cord (illustration). This two-aider system has some benefits, but is more cumbersome than slings.

Russian aid climbers wear a strap system around each ankle and knee to which a hook is attached, slightly below knee level. Their aiders have no steps, rather metal rungs in which the knee hook is inserted as the climber ascends. They claim this knee-hook/aider rung system enables the climber to get higher on a piece than with sewn aiders, though with the system of harness loops described above, I (J.M.) haven't found this to be true. Hanging in the Russian aider set-up feels wobbly at first, and takes some getting used to – should you want to bother.

Clip-in Loops

Clip-in loops tied directly into the harness are essential for proper aider use. On easier aid, a climber need not clip directly into each placement (it is faster if she doesn't); but on the harder, more time-consuming leads, it is most efficient to clip the harness into each piece at successive intervals. This enables the leader to hang directly from the harness, instead of having to stand on her feet all day long with the belayer holding her on tension through the placement.

Picture it: on my harness, along with full-length daisy chains (discussed later), I (J.M.) have two knotted slings which are sized exactly to my personal specs and are tied in the same way the rope is. One loop is sized exactly the length I need to be able to hang from my harness comfortably while in my third step. The third step is where most of the organization and prep for the next placement occurs, such as unclipping the bottom set of aiders and so forth. Once I've got the probable piece for the next placement, I'll climb into the second step, and clip the second knotted loop (shorter than the first) into the piece I'm hanging on. Now my waist is slightly higher than the piece itself, and I'm able to balance out, maximizing my reach for the next placement. If I step higher, into the sub-second loop, or even the top step, carabiners are used to extend the length of my clip-in loop, allowing me to lever out higher from the piece, which is now significantly below my waist (and center of balance). Note that clip-in loops are a convenience: daisy chains clipped off short can be used in place of clip-in loops.

Fifi Hooks

Fifi hooks are used in lieu of a carabiner to connect the climber to the piece. They can be tied into a short sling tied directly from the harness. An optimal length sling will allow you to hang comfortably while the feet are in the third step. Fifi hooks make it easier to hook into the piece for a rest. The downside is that the fifi hook, dangling from the harness, tends to catch on everything. However, for moderate, very overhanging routes like the Leaning Tower, I've (J.L.) found them to be less hassle than using the more elaborate clip-in loops, which come into their own on bleak aid.

Harness with belay loop, one 4-inch supertape loop, one 7-inch supertape loop, and a daisy chain.

Daisy Chains

A daisy chain acts as a secure tentacle – a cord and biner directly connecting the climber to a placement. Daisy chains are made from five-millimeter perlon (knotted) cordage, or sewn, ¾-inch webbing, with loops every foot or so. The overall length extends from your harness to the tip of your reach. Girth hitch the daisy directly into the harness, instead of clipping it in. The girth hitch will never come undone, eliminates the clutter of an extra biner on your harness, and doesn't need to be checked like a carabiner clip-in. For moderate routes, a single daisy is adequate. For harder routes, two separate daisies are useful (different colors).

The usual procedure for moving with aiders, daisies, grab loops, and clip-in loops (with or without fifi) is this:

1. Set placement.
2 Clip a set of aiders to the top piece.
3. Clip daisy to top piece.
4. Test top placement (methods described next).

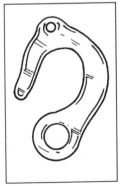

Fifi hook

Wall harness is set up
with two daisy chains
and a fifi hook.

5. Move onto top piece, using grab loop on the aider for balance.

6. Clip rope into bottom piece.

7. Retrieve aiders and daisy from bottom piece.

8. Climb up to second step, or sub-second step; clip-in from your harness, and prepare to place the next piece.

9. Repeat.

TESTING PLACEMENTS: THE FINE POINTS

A good camming unit in a perfect crack is clearly bomber and doesn't need to be tested. Dubious placements, however, should always be tested. The standard method is the bounce test. Properly done, most placements can be tested to handle a small shock load. The theory here is that each piece is tested to withstand body weight, plus the additional force generated by a short, one-placement fall – in case the top piece rips.

To bounce test, clip an aider (and daisy) into the piece to be tested, step into the lowest rung of the aider, slowly apply body weight (checking for shifting), then bounce – slowly at first, gradually building up to forces exceeding body weight. Do not look at the tested placement, since if it does pull, it could strike your face. A good bounce test will generate at least twice the climber's body weight, and should prove or disprove that the piece is adequate for a short (one-placement) fall. It is important not to clip the rope into the piece being tested, since it accomplishes nothing except to make your belayer do more work, as well as lengthening your fall potential. Of major importance, of course, is preventing the present piece from getting shock-loaded if the tested piece does pull. This may require getting well below the tested piece, and to test via connection to the daisy.

In this case, downclimb the previous set of aiders, and clip the daisy into the aider on the test piece. Test by first slowly applying body weight, then bouncing on the daisy connection. *Always stay low* and be tightly connected (with the other daisy) to the previous piece, in case the tested piece pulls. And take care that all your weight is on the tested piece. On the third ascent of the Wyoming Sheep Ranch, in an effort to move fast and make the Cyclops Eye bivy that day, I (J. M.) didn't bother to downclimb to test a sketchy hook placement. The hook I was testing popped, and I fell a few inches onto a large flake that I was also hooked on. The large flake blew, and I pitched off for a 60-foot, head-first whistler, ripping out rivets and copperheads along the way. On my way back up, I had to hook the rivet holes, then work out an intricate alternative around the now missing flake. When in doubt, get low to test.

Sometimes a marginal piece cannot or should not be tested, or can only be mini-tested (for example, long sideways placements, some roof placements, fragile hook placements, and so on). Here, the "ease-onto-it" method requires a monk's faith and a thief's luck.

Testing in the midst of a string of dicey placements is one of the scariest parts of difficult aid climbing; for pitches A3 and above, extensive and proper testing methods are the only means of staying healthy. For now, however, on moderate routes, a good simple weight test in the proper direction of pull is all that's required.

Dave Katz carries an El Cap rack.

Bob Gaines photo

THE RACK

Before you can lead an aid pitch, you need to organize an appropriate rack. An aid pitch may require anything from a handful of biners and wired stoppers (as needed for a bolt or rivet ladder), to the full gamut of gear, including multiple sets of camming units, 50 or more pitons, and about everything else you can buy at a climbing shop or borrow from friends. The key is to carry only what you need, and nothing more. This requires experience and a good eye for viewing the line; so at the outset, take too much rather than too little.

Gear selection is an art. I've (J.M.) seen many teams pour over their gear like warriors tuning their weapons before battle, scrutinizing each piece carefully, and making selections based on weight, size range, function and juju. Each item has a particular use, and though often there are alternatives for each placement, there is usually an optimal piece, based on security, minimal impact on the rock, ease of removal, and calculation on what should be saved for higher on the pitch (for example, you don't use all your #4 Friends if there's a wide section overhead).

A typical clean-climbing aid rack includes 2 to 2½ sets of camming units, 1 or 2 sets of stoppers and brass nuts, plenty of slings and quick draws, and plenty of extra, or "free" biners. The Nose on El Capitan (an all-clean, mostly free big wall) for example, requires 35 to 45 free carabiners. Check the topo, and grill friends who have recently done the route to further dial in the rack.

Slings

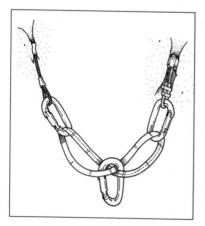

Two anchors equalized with a shoulder-length sling.

Several types of slings are used for aid climbing. A nailing route may require anywhere from 25 to 50 tie-offs, with perhaps half again that number in slightly longer keeper slings. Though strong enough, tie-off loops are prone to fray and are easily weakened by hammer blows. Expect to lose a few for a climb of any length.

"Hero loops" are short supertape slings made from approximately 32 inches of supertape, tied with a water knot. They are versatile; they can be used to extend a piece the length of a carabiner (when doubled), or to tie through the eye of a piton to save having to clip two biners into each piton. Sometimes you'll climb a pitch which is pitons all the way. When you're looking at a 140-foot pitch, averaging even a generous four feet between placements, that means 35 placements. Clipping two biners into each placement means having to haul a rack with 70 free biners. Hero loops can halve this load. They also greatly diminish rope drag, and keep the system fluid and flexible – a much better way all around.

Hero loops are racked on a biner and clipped onto the rack. Keep the biner gate so it opens down and out, for easy access. A clean wall will require few hero loops; for a nailing route, it's nice to have at least 30 of these.

Shoulder-length slings are used to reduce rope drag, save biners, prevent the rope from going over sharp edges, and to equalize belay anchors. Carrying slings on the rack (instead of around the shoulder) is convenient as it keeps them out of the way, yet fairly accessible. Ten to fifteen full-length slings, made from 1-inch webbing or ⅝-inch supertape, should be more than ample for most routes.

Though perhaps premature to mention, be aware of sharp edges while leading, both for yourself and for your partner (who will be jumaring on those edges – explained in detail later on). Slings usually solve this problem, but infrequently, an edge will be so nasty that an article of clothing must be shed and left securely over the edge. If this cannot be accomplished, you'll have to hammer the edge off – bad business, but better than dying.

At belays, it's standard practice to equalize anchors with regular-length, 1-inch slings. Proper equalization distributes the load equally between two anchors, and is secure even if one of the two anchors fail. (For an in-depth look at anchors, read *Climbing Anchors,* also part of the *How To Rock Climb* series).

Double-length slings are good items for the aid arsenal. It is often possible to sling a large block for part of a belay. Two double length slings, knotted and tied up into a tight bundle (carried on a biner on the rack), are sufficient for most climbs. Double-length slings are also handy for rigging a complicated belay, where many marginal placements are equalized in a way to establish a single solid anchor.

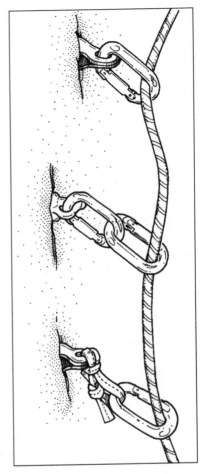

Use of supertape hero loop to keep the rope running smoothly and reduce the use of carabiners.

Top: bad use of one biner – binds rope.
Middle: Two biners – better.
Bottom: Hero loop works best.

Cheater Sticks

Though cheater sticks are fashioned in various ways (all homemade), they generally consist of hooks taped to the end of a long stick or rod, like the shaft of a golf club. Attached to the hook is a loop of sling or webbing that runs (normally duct-taped) down the length of the stick to where you are holding it at the end. The notion is that you can reach past desperate, marginal placements to clip off a bolt, rivet, or some other piece of fixed gear above. In short, a cheater stick allows a leader to skip the last one or two placements before a piece of fixed gear. I (J.L.) saw an Italian team that had a cheater stick made from a marlin rod – the sucker was easily eight feet long – but I don't know if they ever actually used it. Though some consider cheater sticks unethical, it's all part of the game.

TRAIL LINE

Most aid climbing requires a trail line. This is a second line, usually a 9 millimeter rope, attached to a clip-in loop on the back of a climber's harness. The trail line enables the belayer and climber to remain connected at all times. The trail line is also the haul line when hauling is necessary. It's also used to send up additional gear to the leader, should she need any throughout the pitch. It's impractical to carry, on every single lead, all the gear required for a multi-pitch route. At the beginning of each pitch, the rack is pared down to include only what is necessary. No need to take a rack of big cams for a knifeblade crack. On an aid pitch which requires a lot of gear, it is not uncommon for the climber to haul additional gear several times per pitch.

Remember, after the climber is half a rope length out, a third line is necessary to connect to the trail line, since there is not enough rope to both haul up fresh gear and still leave enough line for the belayer to hang onto the end. From a hanging belay several pitches up, forget about letting the end go in the hopes that the climber can toss the trail line back to the belayer. That's usually about as probable as finding an arrowhead on the moon. Once the trail line gets away from you – flapping out there in the breeze some yards out in open space – you're looking at all kinds of tedious shenanigans to try and retrieve it. More on trail lines in Chapter 7: Multi-pitch Routes.

Leading

Practicing aid on free-climbing cracks with Friends, nuts, and clean gear is a good way to wire up the basics (as well as following such pitches with ascenders). Again, do not practice nailing techniques at a free-climbing area. The main objective for your first few aid leads is to get familiar with the motion and sequence of efficient ascent, and working out the system so the basics become second nature: placing, testing, and hanging on gear. For someone used to free-climbing, the slowness of aid may unnerve you at first.

Remember, to stay motivated for aid climbing, you must aid climb – not just study this manual and yak about it. To scale the truly big rocks of the world requires expertise in aid climbing techniques, period. Practicing aid routes on small crags is the first step for sharpening your skills for the big routes.

The basic procedure for moving from one piton, nut, etc. to the next, was already discussed in the section on aid slings. Beyond that, there is little to add about the individual steps. Putting it all together is just a matter of going out and doing so.

Safety

When you're ready to start, you've got a sturdy belayer and sturdy, comfortable shoes. The lead line is tied in, the trail line clipped behind, and it's time to make that first placement. Scan the crack for a good placement at a high reach level, and make the placement. The first pitch off the ground is potentially the most dangerous, owing to the ground fall potential, so it's essential to make solid placements early on.

Consider wearing a helmet for aid pitches. Besides the benefits of head protection in case of a fall, or from falling rock or gear, the helmet also saves the bean from the failure of a tested piece in progress. Also, whenever nailing, and especially when cleaning pitons, it's advisable to wear safety glasses or sunglasses of some kind. A sliver of chrome-moly steel in your eye can be extremely painful and jeopardize your chances of continuing the ascent safely (not to mention jeopardizing your eyesight).

THE NECESSARY BAG OF SKILLS

Cleverness is an asset on aid pitches. Good judgment and innovative thinking are in constant demand. Besides the main challenge of climbing efficiently, an aid pitch offers a continual set of minor challenges, each one unique, and each one requiring a slightly different solution. With experience, one learns the "tricks of the trade" (mostly through trial and

Wearing a helmet should be considered an essential piece of aid climbing equipment

Evetree Erdman on Moonlight Buttress, Zion.

Bill Hatcher photo

error), and the complex task of aid climbing becomes natural. One develops an eye for a placement, an innate ability to deal with multiple ropes, slings, aiders, pins, biners, and so on, plus an awareness of the interrelationship among the climbing gear, the stone, and upward progress.

While preparing for an aid lead, first study the line and mentally calculate a general plan: how slings will be running in order to minimize rope drag, and how, for example, a certain piece of gear should be saved for a section above. Overall efficiency is the name of the game, and accurate judgment is required.

It is one thing to understand the system, quite another to perform it without a hitch. So expect considerable fumbling and crossed ropes and countless other bumblings until you've executed the procedures over and over. The smoothness and efficiency of a wall ace hinges in large part on his or her ability to predict the snagged line or the rope drag before the fact. And this kind of anticipation can only come with experience.

However frazzled and disorganized things might get at the outset, as long as you make certain the placements are sound (test them well), and that the lead line is clipped in correctly, there is no real jeopardy. The system gets automatic very quickly, so patience those first few times out is essential.

Virtually all aid climbing, even for the expert, is a constant struggle with organization, requiring fixed vigilance to keep track of the myriad of slings, aiders, gear, crossed lines and multiple ropes. If you stay organized, half the battle is won. If you try a piece for a placement, say, and it doesn't fit, take the extra second and re-rack it in its proper place. Consistency in keeping the aider and daisy not in use in a specific, out-of-the-way place (usually clipped onto the rack) will help keep things clean and ordered. Eventually, the mechanics will grow more and more natural, and the essence of the climbing will shine through the epics of organization.

Route Finding

Believe it: on complicated aid pitches it is possible to "get lost," to climb the wrong feature or crack only to find yourself in the middle of nowhere. Like when my (J.L.) friends Hal Stokker and Frank "The Mouth" Sims were bagging the second ascent of the Bridwell/-Faint route on Washington Column. Up high the cracks are flaky and nondescript. With few piton scars to mark the way, and in his haste to get on with it, the Mouth went and headed up the wrong crack. He quickly found himself strung way out on desperate terrain, hooking and weeping shamelessly. In half an hour he was well-nigh had, for he was already more than half a rope length out, and could no longer lower back to the belay and start over. Nor did he want to down-clean the pitch, for most every placement was bogus. He finally took a fifty-foot screamer when a block came off in his hands. Then he had enough rope to lower back to the belay. He also had a ten-stitch gash in his noggin and a memory that would lay hold of him in the still of the night.

The point is – look where you're going before you cast off. On well-traveled routes, there are always signs of previous ascents: fixed gear, pin scars, and so on. If there appears to be more than one way to go, check the topo. If that doesn't clear things up, study the options carefully, and take the most straightforward-looking route. Most false starts or dead ends have retreat slings a ways up the pitch. Look for these, and steer clear. Always keep your eyes open, and check your bearings.

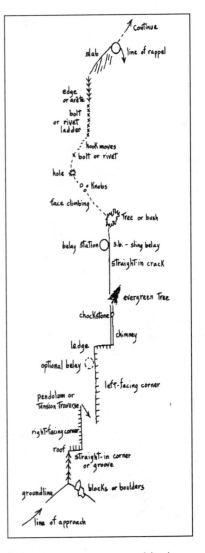

Common guidebook route topo symbol key, this one from Yosemite Climbs

Tension Traverses and Pendulums

On some steep aid pitches you must sometimes traverse to another crack. Often you can aid across, sometimes free climb across; but more often than not, aid from the rope is required. With a tension traverse, the belayer pays out rope on demand from the leader, lowering her from a high point and holding her on a tensioned rope. This allows the climber to semi-free climb across the rock via tension from the line (that is up and off to the side). Because the rope takes so much of the leader's weight, only the scantiest holds are required to move sideways. A tension traverse is normally performed when you need to gain a feature almost directly to the side, or even slightly up. The angle of the rock and the available features determine what you can do. If it's steep and blank, you'll have to pendulum.

John Middendorf on a difficult pendulum on the first ascent of the Kali-Yuga, Half Dome.

A pendulum requires full weighting of the rope, and you'll normally run back and forth across the face to order to gain sufficient momentum to sprint/swing across to another crack or feature. Sometimes you must have a hook handy to pull onto a flake; other times a final lunge will launch you into a desperate free climbing maneuver. Though rarely, a climber will find a suave hand crack at the end of the pendulum (as on the stove-legs pendulum on The Nose, El Cap).

Understand that whether you tension or pendulum or hook sideways, you must have some feature – some crack, knob, flake, or some such thing – to aim for. Sometimes, though rarely, you must swing blindly around a corner, hoping for pay dirt. In either case, lower down a little at a time, and feather out the slack as you find that you need it, as opposed to lowering down too much, then having to reclimb the lower placements or jumar the rope to regain altitude. Close and exact communication with the belayer is essential, for a foot too much slack (or too little) can mean the difference between reaching that flake or crack, and swinging back empty-handed.

Always study just what you're swinging for, and what manner of climbing will follow, making certain you have the appropriate gear on your rack. On a new route on Mt. Watkins, we were nearing the top after five days of broiling our asses off on the great ivory face. I (J.L.) could almost smell the summit, and the waiting stream, and was so anxious to execute a difficult pendulum and top out that I didn't bother to eyeball the climbing that followed it. At the end of my swing, a severe grab and mantle was followed by harsh face climbing

Commands for pendulums

OK, TENSION: Belayer takes in slack and holds.

HOLD ME HERE: Belayer locks off the belay.

LOWER ME: Belayer lowers climber.

SLACK, SLOW: Belayer gives slack slowly, usually coordinating slack payout with climber's motions (usually when climber is free climbing under tension after the pendulum).

LOTS OF SLACK: Belayer gives lots of slack and resumes regular belay, usually after leader reaches a stance or good protection.

into a flared pod. I didn't have the one nut I needed, was already too far out to haul it up, and was left to carry on via rude arm-barring. After thirty feet of unprotected 5.10, the pod pinched off to a shallow gash, and I had to start aiding on a string of placements so scandalous that the first one ripped three times when I tested it, all the while swiveling from a sketchy arm bar and looking at an eighty footer. Bridwell said in his whole life he'd only seen one other man's legs shake so bad, and that man had dengue fever. Keep your eyes peeled, and go prepared.

Free Climbing

A leader must sometimes free climb a section after aiding. To leave the security of the aiders is exciting work, especially when the aiders must be retrieved for future use, as is the case with "mixed" climbing (mixed = free and aid on the same lead). There are many considerations. Overlook one crucial factor, and you'll find yourself naked in a hailstorm.

As with pendulums, when you step out of your aid slings and onto free climbing, you need a plan before you go for it. Scope out the climbing above. You'll most likely be carrying more gear than you normally would when free climbing, so try to reckon what gear you will need to protect yourself above, and organize that gear for quick and easy access. Maybe have the first piece ready. If the way is clear – say you are leaving a rivet ladder and face climbing to a three-bolt belay – leave some, if not most all of the aid gear at the top aid rivet, so you are less encumbered for the free section. Remember, of course, to bring enough gear to rig the belay. If the free section is short, and is followed by more aid, you'll have to take everything with you. You'll still want to take a hard look at the free climbing, assess what you'll need for protection, get that pro ready, and get slings and gear moved toward your backside so you don't trip or get hung up on anything (clip daisies and spare aiders out of the way). There are various ways to go about things, but the process is basically as follows:

On the last point of aid, get up high in one aid ladder (the others having been clipped off to your harness, out of the way), get the hold or jam above, step out of the last aider, set your feet on holds or in jams, unclip the aider from the placement and clip it off to your harness or rack – and have at the free climbing. If the free section is long and hard, leave a short sling at the last aid point, using it as an aid sling. This frees you up from having to reach back down and unclip the aid sling (grim duty if you're hanging off a crimper) and also allows you (while still standing in the sling) to bunch the aiders into smaller loops by clipping the aid sling biner into a couple of lower rungs. This way, you won't have to trail a long aider clipped to your harness, which will invariably get hung up on either a foot or a hold.

By far the diciest (and thankfully, rarest) scenario is the one described in the pendulum section, when you leave a long string of shaky aid placements and jump straight onto ghastly, poorly-protected free climbing. The same considerations we've just laid down apply here, but you'd better take a few moments longer to scope out the difficulties overhead, and get yourself well organized for one of the scariest maneuvers in all of rock climbing. Such extreme mixed climbing is strictly experts' ground, and is virtually never encountered on standard wall climbs.

On the final pitch of Never Never Land on the first solo ascent of the route, I (J.M.) spotted what I thought would be moderate free climbing to the right of the difficult and awkward-looking final A4 seam. After 30 feet of free climbing, I found myself committed on a narrow mantle ledge with no pro. After a long while pondering the final 10 feet (wishing I were on the relatively safer A4 section to my left), I finally moved through the do-or-die 5.10c section, fired by adrenaline. Always scope carefully before committing to free climbing.

A vertical belay is simple to set up, but crams everything together, making good organization essential.

Belay Set-ups

Once the belay is reached, concentrate on keeping things organized, for the rigging grows increasingly complex – and quickly. In rigging belays, visualize where your partner will be coming up, where you'll haul from, and where you'll be hanging while your partner leads the next pitch. When the anchors are spread out, belay set-ups are simple; when the anchors are bunched together or stacked vertically, proficient rigging can be tricky.

Chaos at the belay!
Bob Gaines photo

Always check your own, the haulbag's, and your partner's connection to the belay. Sometimes in the confusion of constructing a solid belay, things can be overlooked or unclipped. Not good.

As mentioned, *Climbing Anchors* is devoted entirely to the subject of protection and anchoring systems, and if we tried

Horizontal belay setups help keep gear organized, but the individual anchors are harder to equalize.

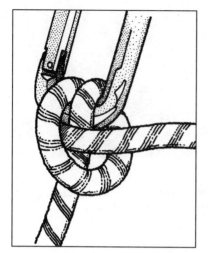

to incorporate that material here, this manual would be thicker than Durant's *The Story of Civilization*. But let's look at some practical routines particular to wall climbing.

Tie the rope directly into the most solid anchor points of the belay (at least two or three times). Most wall experts prefer clove hitches, which are easy to adjust. The drawback is that the clove hitch uses most of the U part of the biner, and so allows only one clip in per biner. Figure eights are good, but are difficult to adjust. Normally, belays will be tied in with a combination of clove hitches and figure eights, the figure eight normally used on the top, bombproof piece.

As a side note, understand that it's always possible to construct a more bombproof belay; but if you ever hope to get up a wall, you don't have the time to make a science project out of every belay station, or to try to fabricate some obtuse matrix an engineer has designed on graph paper. The task is to construct a belay

Above, a clove hitch.

To the right, a typical belay rigged with both clove hitches and figure eight knots.

that, without a doubt, will do the job and do it well. The belay must be inviolate, and far more hefty than a normal free climbing belay anchor because of the greatly increased loads, and, in the event of hard nailing, the possibility of long falls. This does not mean you need an anchor good to 50,000 pounds, rather one that will never rip out no matter the falls it must hold.

Whatever anchor you end up with, tie in with enough slack to be able to haul (the mechanics of which are discussed in Chapter 8) – normally eight to ten feet of slack, if the pitch is not a rope-stretcher. Hang from a jumar attached to the anchored rope and clipped directly into your harness (this jumar will also be used for hauling.) The maneuverability you get from the extra slack helps with hauling, and allows down-jumaring to retrieve items from the haulbags. (Jumaring is discussed in detail in the next chapter.) Make sure that the slack can be removed if the next pitch is a rope- stretcher. Daisies can be clipped into the belay as a backup.

Whenever possible, equalize anchors with regular-length one-inch slings. Proper equalization distributes the load equally between two or more anchors, and is secure even if one of the anchors blows.

After finishing the pitch, rigging the belay and hauling the pack and/or haulbag, it's time to settle in while your partner finishes cleaning the pitch. Get comfortable. Streamline and reorganize everything you can, thinking about the crowding that will result when your partner comes up and re-racks the gear. Get ready for belaying, and keep the ropes untangled and running smoothly as the leader heads off on the next pitch. It's the belayer's job to facilitate the leader in any way he can – in sending up gear, making sure the trail line does not snag, etc. The various maxims set down in *Climbing Anchors* are required knowledge for anyone heading onto a big wall.

Nailing Leads

For nailing pitches, the techniques are the same as for all-clean pitches, except that more gear (heavy gear at that) is needed, requiring more vigilance to organization.

Take a typical aid pitch on Mescalito (El Capitan). The rack may consist of 3 sets of camming units to #3, 2 sets to #4, one oversize camming device (#5 or #7), 2-3 sets of stoppers and brass nuts, 25 to 50 pitons of various sizes, lots of full-length slings and hero loops, tie-offs, hooks and other many other gadgets – plus up to 80 free carabiners. The particular wall will determine the amount of pitons required. In general, if the route has many ascents, fewer pitons are needed. A generic pin rack for a trade route consists of several birdbeaks, 2 or 3 Leeper Z-tons, 5 to 10 knifeblades, 12 to 18 Lost Arrows, 3 or 4 each Baby

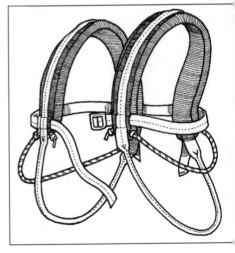

A double gear sling distributes the weighty equipment much more comfortably.

Gear loads on El Cap. Steve Quinlan on Tribal Rite.

John Middendorf photo

Angles (½-inch and ⅝-inch), 2 to 3 ¾-inch angles, 1 to 2 each 1-inch, 1¼-inch, and 1½-inch angles, and perhaps a bong (for luck).

It cannot be overstated: proper organization while preparing a nailing lead is essential. The "double gear sling" is the ticket for heavier racks. With these, racking has become both simple and comfortable, for no longer is the climber strangled by gear slings crisscrossing his neck. Two padded slings sit on each shoulder, connected in the back and front. The most versatile have two loops on each side (for maximum organization), and strong tie-in loops for clipping the entire rack in. A tip: rack pins (five to six knifeblades per biner, four to five Lost Arrows per biner, three to four baby angles per biner, and two to three angles per biner), slings, and tie-offs on the right side; Friends, wired tapers, copperheads, and hooks on the left side, or vice versa. Then distribute the free biners so as to equalize the weight on each side. However you rack up, quick access requires a consistent, familiar system.

Leapfrogging

Especially with clean gear, you'll want to sometimes remove the previous piece for reuse later on: "leapfrogging." Camming devices are most commonly leapfrogged in a uniform sized crack. Consider leading a 165-foot, one-inch-wide crack with only three or four camming units of that size. Clearly you'll have to leapfrog the units. "Backcleaning" is similar to leapfrogging, but entails lowering off a solid piece to retrieve pieces farther below than the next lower piece.

Following Pitches

Once a pitch is led, the belayer will switch from the role of holding the rope and general facilitator of the leader, to the role of "cleaner." She'll clip her belay device away, unclip the haulbag, attach her jumars and prepare to clean the gear as she ascends to the belay. Let's first look at some of the specific equipment used for the task.

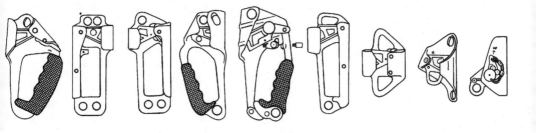

Ascenders

There are various brands of ascenders. All are mechanical devices that clip onto the rope; aid slings are clipped through a hole in the bottom of the ascender. When your weight is shifted onto the aider/ascender, a toothed cam clamps against the line, preventing the unit from slipping down. When unweighted, the unit can be pushed up the rope by hand. You ascend by pushing and stepping up alternately between the two ascenders/aiders. The action closely resembles someone working out on a stair machine. A weighted ascender cannot be moved up. Most ascenders are very durable, but they do wear out; routinely inspect them after each wall, especially around the cam. Because Jumar ascenders were the first ones used in Yosemite, all ascenders are often referred to as jumars; likewise, ascending a rope is commonly called jumaring (or jugging), no matter the brand of ascender used.

There are four main types of ascenders: Jumar, Clog, CMI, and Petzl. Choosing among them is a matter of personal preference. Petzls are superior for frozen ropes, while many consider Clogs the most comfortable. The traditional yellow Jumars are the heaviest, but have the big advantage of being workable with either hand (whereas the others are all set up for the right or left hand exclusively).

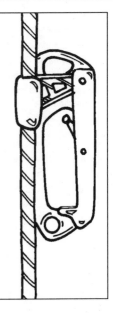

Make sure the safety catch is always engaged!

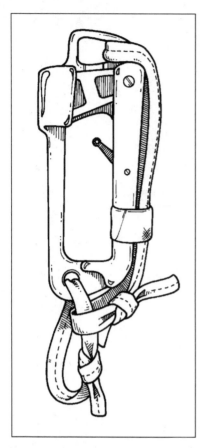

Rigging jumars

Note: it is also possible to rig so that both loops can be clipped.

Each brand has its pros and cons, but any of the four mentioned are well-suited for big wall climbing. Another type of ascender has a hinged handle which is connected directly to the cam, applying a force on the rope which is directly proportional to the weight being applied. Although not as strong as traditional ascenders, hinged-handle ascenders work the best on iced or muddy ropes.

THE SET-UP

Clip one aider onto each ascender with a locking biner. Clip daisies directly from the harness to each ascender into the locking biner. To avoid an extra biner, girth hitch the daisy directly into the harness. A big advantage of doing so is that you never have to check if the daisy is clipped in. The daisy connection to the jumars are the cleaner's principal "belay," so make certain the system is foolproof.

You must always remained clipped into both jumars with daisies. Decide whether you'd like your right or left ascender higher. If you are right-handed, your right hand goes higher (top hand), as it will be clipped on and off the rope more frequently as you clean. This requires some dexterity, so the more coordinated hand should be on top.

When the top ascender is slightly below full arm extension (you don't want to be stretching to reach it), the daisy to the ascender must be tight. That is, at a comfortable arm's reach of the upper jumar, the climber can rest on his harness via the daisy. The most common mistake first time wall climbers make is to have the wrong-sized daisy connecting them to the top jumar. If it's too short, you can't get a full arm's extension, and are left to "jug" with quick little strokes (also known as "short-dicking" the rope). If the daisy is too long, you cannot lean back on the ascender, and are left to hang off your top hand, which will flame out quickly and thoroughly.

The length of the bottom daisy to the lower ascender isn't so crucial, but it shouldn't be *too* long. This daisy will catch you if you fall out of your aiders and your top ascender comes off the rope. This rarely happens, but the point is, the bottom daisy is your only belay when you are clipping the top ascender over a placement.

Final and most important for efficiently ascending a vertical wall (for right-handed folks; reverse for south paws): step the right foot into the third step of the higher aider, and the left foot into the second step of the lower aider. This is not obvious at first, until you see that it equalizes the length at which the feet lie (since the lower ascender is generally below the top ascender by approximately a loop length of an aider). On lower-angle turf, the length of the top daisy should be increased, since your chest will be farther away from the rope and the ascender than it would be on steeper terrain. The right foot is placed in the fourth step of the top aider, and the left foot in the third step of the lower aider. The point is to keep the feet one step apart in the aiders.

When jumaring horizontal sections, clip a biner into the bottom of the handle and into the rope. This keeps oblique pressures from torquing the unit off the rope. Lastly, never bounce, which stresses the anchor unnecessarily, and can saw the sheath of the rope if it's running over even the slightest edge.

Your first few efforts jugging a rope are invariably strange and frustrating escapades requiring more energy to move up than to actually climb the same section of rock. But once you get the daisy lengths dialed in, and become familiar with placing the feet in various steps of the aider and the required weight shifts and motions (there are only a couple), you'll find your rhythm and will be jogging up the rope in no time. Remember that if the top daisy (the one connecting you to the high ascender) is not perfectly adjusted for you, then you'll never get the system down. Remember also that even when everything is right, true mastery of ascenders takes time.

CLEANING PITCHES

As the rope is ascended, the gear that the leader placed must be removed, or "cleaned." It is most efficient to get slightly above the piece being cleaned. This requires moving the top jumar (or "jug") past the carabiner connecting the placement to the rope. On perfectly vertical, plumb-line pitches, you simply unclip the rope from the biner. Other times (when the line swerves even slightly), and owing to tension on the rope, the top jumar must be unclipped from the rope and reclipped above the piece. To accomplish this, your weight must be entirely on the lower foot, in the lower aider. You'll find yourself holding onto the lower jumar for support as you unclip the top ascender, reach, and clip it back onto the rope above the placement. The only practical way to unclip an ascender and re-clip it back into the rope is with one hand. Each ascender works a little differently, so you'll want to practice this move on the ground before you try it on a route, getting a firm grasp of how the move is

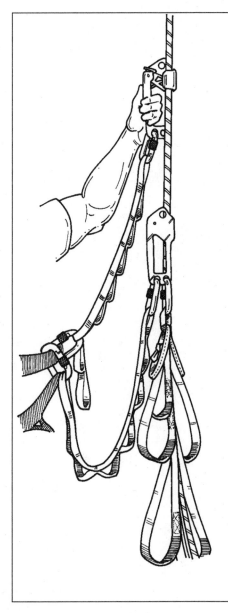

Using daisies with jumars. The proper length to the top jumar is critical.

Proper ascender/daisy/ aider set-up

accomplished – what levers to thumb, and so on. With Jumar brand ascenders, it's an easy move once you've done it a few times. Not so with other ascenders.

The technique of clipping one ascender over a piece also applies to moving over the abrupt lip of a ledge. Always check, recheck, and check again the status of the safety catch on your jumar. If it is not in place, the ascender will slip off the rope. John Booth recently took a 100-foot whipper on the Zodiac, El Capitan, burning his hands badly in the process, because he assumed his safety catch was engaged as he clipped his ascenders over the sharp edge of a shelf.

Once the top jumar is reclipped above the piece, push it as high as possible, then sit back on your daisy in the rest position. Resist the temptation to hang on the top jumar with your arm. It will flame out in one pitch if you do.

Once your weight is totally on the upper jumar, you can unclip the rope from the piece. If the crack is even slightly off plumb, you'll have to take your weight off the lower jumar/- aider to get slack to unclip. Everyone does things a little differently, but most climbers push both jumars a few feet above the now unclipped piece, one jug just below the other. If the line is straight up and down, and the piece is a piton, spread your legs so the peg is between your two aiders, at about stomach level. With your aiders out of the way and jumars well above, you have a nice little space to wield the hammer. Remove the biner(s) and any hero loop. For speed, most climbers then clip in a cleaning biner (described previously), and pulling on the sling connected to it, slam the pin in earnest. Usually only a couple blows are necessary to work even a buried pin loose, and you can yank it out by yarding on the cleaning biner while smacking it a couple more times. Nuts are usually removed by leaving the biner on them and simply pulling them out.

It is particularly important to re-rack the free biners in one group, and the nuts and pitons according to size as you go. If you simply clip stuff off wherever, you'll have to sort the whole chaos out once you reach the belay; and if your partner doesn't smack you for shoddy racking, she should. An efficient cleaner keeps things organized, so the two racks (the leading rack and the gear you have just cleaned) can be blended quickly once the belay is reached.

You might have realized that as you jumar up the rope, in effect you have three "belays." Two are supplied by the jumars themselves. The fact that you are tied into the end of

the rope creates the third belay. However, if for some fluke reason both jumars come unclipped from the rope, you're going to fall all the way until you hit the end of the line. If you've already jumared and cleaned half a pitch, say, that's a very long way to fall. To safeguard against taking such a colossal whistler – should both jumars fail – you simply tie

Lisa Raleigh following the third pitch of Speak No Evil, The Three Gossips, Arches National Park.

Duane Raleigh photo

Clipping over a piece

into the rope as you go. This is a very easy and quick procedure, and takes about five seconds once you get it down.

You tie into your main harness biner with a loop (overhand knot is fine) every forty feet, or whenever you feel like it. (Note: when climbing on fixed ropes, this may not be possible if you want to keep both ends of the rope tied into anchors.) Since you won't want to be dragging too many loops behind you, unclip (and untie) the previous knot after you have replaced it with a new one.

If you're cleaning a straight up-and-down lead on a smooth wall, there is little chance of both jumars coming off the rope, and I'll (J.L.) only clip in a few times when cleaning the entire pitch. If you are traversing a lot, unclipping the top jumar in awkward positions, you'll want to tie in more frequently. On clean rock in mild conditions (where the rope is not iced up), this procedure is as much for peace of mind as it is for anything else because, in reality, the probability of a vigilant cleaner having both jugs blow off the line is about the same as Noah's Ark washing up on Waikiki. But through both bad luck and faulty technique, both ascenders have come off a line and have caused fatal accidents, so virtually every experienced wall climber ties into the rope as he cleans – as a matter of course. During the hundreds of leads I've (J.L.) cleaned on jumars, I've never had even one ascender blow off the rope.

Securing a jumar on a horizontal rope

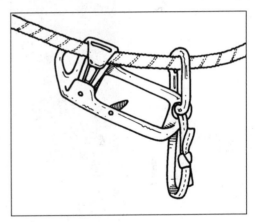

And remember: jumar smoothly. Never bounce.

Cleaning Roofs, Traverses, and Pendulums

One of the trickiest aspects of cleaning is following the rope over roofs and across traverses (the techniques are the same). When the next piece is way off to the side, for instance, it's impossible to fully weight the top jumar (clipped above a piece to be cleaned) because the bottom jumar will be sucked up into the bottom piece before the top piece is fully weighted. This happens when the leader has either tension-traversed or pendulumed from a piece, or when a long sideways reach was made. One technique is for the

Sue McDevitt jumaring on the Wall of Early Morning Light, El Capitan.

Dan McDevitt photo

cleaner to reclimb the placements with a separate set of aiders (pushing the ascenders along as you go): you may clip an extra aider into the next piece, stand in it, and clean the previous piece. This gets dicey if the placements are slim, but when they're solid, this is a suitable method. Generally, however, all the climber's weight is suspended continually from the jumar/aider/daisy system with the techniques we've just covered. The most frequently used method is to clip the top jumar as high as possible on the rope – above the piece – then use both hands to manipulate the rope through the bottom jumar: one to feed the rope below the bottom jumar, the other to manually open the cam on the bottom jumar. It is necessary to equalize the weight by pulling the rope below the jumar with sufficient force to enable the cam to be opened manually. Then, with the cam open, slowly lower yourself out by feeding the rope through. It is difficult to visualize the mechanics of this process, but a study of the illustrations on the next two pages should make it clear enough.

For cleaning longer traverses, the cleaner/follower must often lower off an anchor. This anchor is usually fixed. If not, you must leave it. The anchor can be anything from a fixed stopper, to a slung horn, to a fixed copperhead. There are two methods to lower off a piece, depending on the length of the traverse. The simplest, quickest way to clean short pendulums (long ones must be rappelled) is the "Deucy Method": 1) Grab a bight (loop) of rope; 2) Pass it through the pendulum point sling; 3) Clip the bight into a biner in the harness; 4) Pull the slack out of the bight so the weight is on the bight and off the jumars; 5) Unclip the pendulum point biner, and lower out (only one hand is necessary). The rope will pull through the pendulum point sling after lowering (unclip bight from harness and pull through).

A sportier method involves hanging from the cleaning biner (clipped from your harness to the piece), and hammering away at the pendulum point piece until it pulls; a sudden swing ensues. Although sometimes performed on short traverses on very steep and smooth rock, this technique is not recommended. Be careful not to do what Gordy Smail did on the first attempt of Cosmos. Not wanting to leave a knifeblade, he proceeded to lower onto a marginal piece, and after cleaning the semi-bomber blade he could have lowered from, he ripped the next 60 feet of gear – on a downward slanting traverse. The ensuing 100 foot whipper/-swing flayed the hide off all ten of his knuckles, and rattled him enough that the ascent was postponed.

Cleaning long pendulums

To clean a long pendulum, such as the swing into the "Hollow Flake" (Salathé Wall, El Capitan), a rappel of some sort must be rigged up, allowing you to rappel off the same piece of protection that the leader pendulumed off. If an extra rope is available (it rarely is), a separate rappel can be set by rigging a doubled rope through the anchor. If only one rope is available, the climber cleaning the pitch must first tie into the rope as short as possible, then untie from the end of the rope. The extra line – that which is left between where the leader is tied off and the end of the rope – is used to rig the rappel. This is a simple procedure, but very difficult to render intelligible in words. Study the illustration, then return to this description.

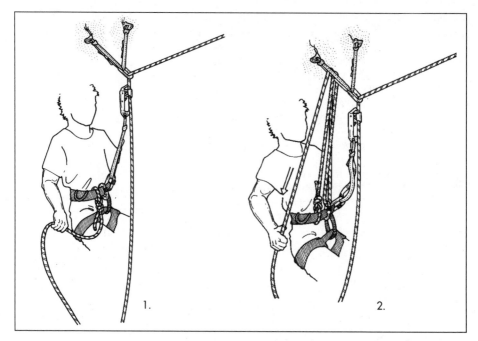

The Duecy Method of cleaning short pendulums.

Of crucial importance here – and indeed, any time you untie from the end of the rope – is to make certain to heed these points: 1) On any big wall, you'll always want to be tied into the rope in one fashion or another. In the above-mentioned scenario, you must tie in above the end, using a bight (loop) of rope, and clipping this bight off to your harness. The preferred knot to tie into the middle of the rope is a figure eight on a bight. An overhand knot will do, but it is a dingo to untie once it's been heavily weighted. 2) Never clip the bight off to your harness using only one carabiner. Use at least two, preferably locking models, gates opposed. 3) Whenever you have to tie off to the middle of the rope, rig the whole works up and doublecheck it before you untie from the end.

How not to go about cleaning a big pendulum is perfectly illustrated by the shocking work of the late, great Tobin Sorrenson, during the first clean ascent of the South Face of Mt. Watkins, in 1975. On the first pitch, the leader ascends a corner, then face climbs out right to a bolt. He then lowers down a very long ways, swings right to another bolt, lowers down again and once again swings far right to the belay. When Tobin was cleaning this pitch and gained the first bolt, rather than rig himself a backline to lower/rappel out on, he simply tied himself off short and jumped, taking an enormous screamer down and over to the next pendulum point. Astonishingly, he repeated the same maneuver on the next pendulum. He might have saved himself a few minutes, but suffered wicked roadburns he would take to his grave, to say nothing of scaring the crap out of his partners. Only your worst enemy would recommend this method.

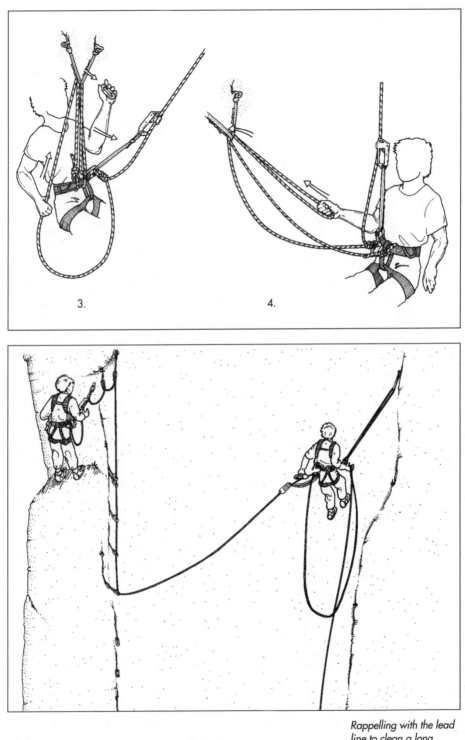

3.

4.

Rappelling with the lead
line to clean a long
pendulum.

CHAPTER 7

Multi-pitch Routes

No matter how aptly we serve up the information here, none of the descriptions take into account that the wall climber must perform his duties a country mile off the deck. And this ingredient is the biggest part of it – make no mistake about that. There is a certain mechanical satisfaction to polishing off a challenging lead, but it is the raw adventure of doing so very far above the trees that gives wall climbing its unique magic. Wall climbing is not for everyone. You will find out soon enough if you belong on a big wall. If you do, the key to enjoyment is to find a partner who is similarly disposed to the high crag.

PICKING A PARTNER

There is no typical climber, and there are no typical climbing partnerships. I've (J.L.) seen fat and skinny teams, men and women, lesbian teams, women dragging their frightened boyfriends behind them, a sergeant in the Israeli special forces and a dentist from Qatar climb Half Dome together. I've met a famous priest and rabbi team on the Troll Wall in Norway, have seen macho teams, teams who would cry at the end of each climb, teams that screamed and ranted the whole while and teams that never exchanged a word. In Yosemite, I knew two wall climbers – one from Puerto Rico, the other from France – who apparently hated each other, who rarely were seen together on the ground and had to be pulled from each other's throats when they were. Yet the two returned to Yosemite for five successive summers, and would never venture onto a big climb without the other. The Frenchman was killed in a car accident in Merced, and the Puerto Rican never got over it and never climbed again. My friend Dean "Bullwinkle" Fidelman twice inveigled girlfriends onto big walls, and at night, in a hammock lashed some thousands of feet up a vertical wall, they'd do their private business, buck naked, with the rope tied only around their ankles! Dean's pants got away from him during one of these trysts, and the next day he had to polish off the route wearing only a breechcloth fashioned from his t-shirt.

Good partnerships normally hinge on both climbers being technically competent and compatible – and many climbers put more stock in the latter than the former. The stress on the high crag can overwhelm, and bitterness toward a partner, who is perceived as dragging his oar through whining and sloth, for instance, can and has demolished

(opposite page)

Xaver Bongard jumaring fixed lines on pitch 21, Sea of Dreams, El Capitan.

Bill Hatcher photo

John Middendorf free climbing the last pitch on the headwall of Tricks of the Tramp, Zion

Bill Hatcher photo

many friendships. I once overheard a team rappelling off the Salathé, and after lots of fierce shouting, a thunderous "*Off rappel, asshole!*" rolled through the air. Just remember that no matter how compatible partners are, minor stresses and awkward times are inevitable, and are, in fact, part of the whole McGilla. Like marriage, the closeness of living and spending so much time together brings out the critic in us all, for there is nowhere to hide on a big wall, and you see all of the other climber, warts included. Big walls are mostly hard labor, like building the pyramids, with a lot a fear and uncertainty thrown in as well. A working partnership is a team who have a mutual understanding of the task at hand and their specific roles in it, and have the willingness and ability to perform. Most things must be understood from the start – that the climbers will swing leads, that each person will do the work of leading a pitch, hauling, and then setting up for a belay session in turn. The conflicts usually come in tasks that are, or should be, shared, like getting the haulbags off the anchor, ferrying loads, exchanging gear, and setting up a bivouac site. Good communication can go far in alleviating differences. A sense of levity – difficult to assert on a wall – and respect for your partner's needs and abilities usually makes for a compatible situation.

Before committing to a week-long epic with someone, consider doing a multi-pitch climb to work out any differences in style or ideas about general procedures. Snags can later be discussed on the ground, long before the team commits to living in each others' laps for upwards of a week. Big walls can make the Pope cranky, so allow for occasional moods. Most importantly, realize that some people talk big on the ground, but in a desperate situation (as so often is found during the course of a big wall climb), can't put their hammer where their mouth was, so to speak. Drive the car before you buy it.

PICKING A ROUTE

Picking a route from the multitude of choices can be confounding. Start on established routes before attempting any of the lesser-known ones. Talk to other climbers. Most climbers in Yosemite, for example, progress through an established pattern of successively more difficult routes. The important thing is not to get too far over one's head, and to have a fair inkling of the challenge involved (based on previous experience), and to be prepared for all contingencies. It normally takes some years to gain the experience to climb a demanding big wall, so start with small bites, and richen the fare as desire and ability dictate. See the appendix for starter routes.

EXPERIENCE AND CONFIDENCE

Good judgement and experience are hard earned. It has been said that good judgement comes from experience, but experience comes from the lack of judgement. The fact is, big walls require considerable acumen to deal with complex systems. An engineer or someone good with puzzles usually does well from the start. Regardless, however, attitude is important.

Big wall climbing is a sport in itself – an adventure requiring specialized gear and techniques, and above all, a specialized state of mind. In fact, the state of mind required for a multi-day big wall ascent is so unique that many are unable to "click into it," and thus the initial failure rate by far exceeds the initial success rate. Commonly, a climber's natural impulse, once on the wall, is to immediately want to go down (intimidation, sudden lack of motivation). If the mind succumbs to this impulse, it can quickly conjure reasons for bailing off. Consequently, many parties retreat without any specific reason, but with stacks of general ones:

weather looked poor, not enough water, bellyache, and all the rest. Generally, if it's possible to push through the first day or two of indecision, the rest is far easier.

A determined and positive perspective is required for a successful big wall ascent; dispassionate or negative attitudes almost ensure failure. Wall climbing requires three basic mental talents: 1) Concentration and awareness: the ability to "keep the lid on" for long periods of time, combined with forethought and a fine-tuned perception of the environment (gear, rock, weather, partner, etc.); 2) Commitment: commitment to achieving a goal, and a willingness to repeatedly make an effort and deal with hardships positively; and 3) Communication: working effectively and efficiently with partners. The mental aspect of big wall climbing is probably more crucial and challenging than the physical fact of hammering your way up the wall.

GENERAL PROCEDURES

As the length of a climb increases, so does its technical complexity. Managing the gear and ropes require constant vigilance; poor management can so bungle the lines that sorting them out can entail more effort than climbing the route. Once more than a pitch off the ground, the danger of dropping things becomes acute, and the consequences become dire. After several pitches, anything dropped is gone for the rest of the route, so it is crucial to keep everything clipped in at all times. Dropping the rack can make both upward and downward progress impossible. You're stuck. And if you can't get a rescue, you're done for.

Most walls require the team to schlep enough gear to outfit a battalion of Marines. It's up to the climber to strategically pick and choose from his arsenal to optimize speed and security in ascending a given section. A typical aid pitch will require up to 50 placements, so husbanding the gear is a real concern. You must be aware, and keep track of, every single item despite the confusion of multiple ropes, cramped belays, and so forth. And at all costs, remain tied in at all times. When untying on a ledge for whatever reason, it's possible to overlook tying back in altogether. It has happened, and the results were not pretty.

CARRYING and HAULING THE PACK

Most multi-pitch aid routes require a pack. If the pack is light enough, or if the terrain is low-angle and unhaulable, the second can carry it as he follows. For most steep routes, however, it's preferred that the leader hauls the pack after she leads the pitch. Many multi-pitch routes require a full day's worth of provisions (12 or more pounds of food and water), emergency rain gear, head lamps, plus a spare rope. Trying to clean an intricate aid pitch with all that crap on your back is miserable duty.

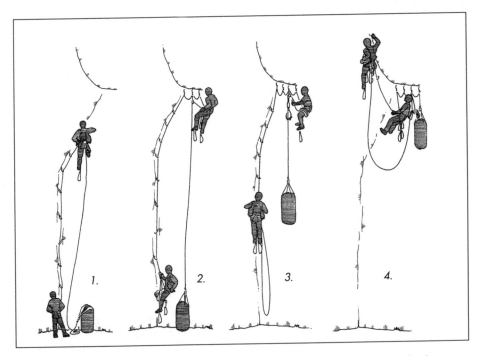

BASIC SYSTEMS

The basic wall system requires three ropes: a lead line (a sturdy 11-millimeter), a haul line (9-millimeter to 11-millimeter), and a lower-out line (9-millimeter preferred – optional for many routes).

Picture this: Buzz and Woody on a "big stone." 1) Buzz leads, Woody belays. 2) Buzz finishes pitch, sets up new belay, prepares to haul. 3) After Buzz has hauled up all of the slack on the haul line – plus a little more to unweight the bag – Woody releases haulbag from his belay station (if need be, lowering it out with the lower-out line), and Buzz hauls it. 4) Woody cleans pitch (jumaring); meanwhile, Buzz finishes hauling and organizes the ropes at the belay. 5) Woody arrives at Buzz's belay, prepares to lead. 6) Woody leads, Buzz belays. Repeat until dark (bivy), or until topped out.

With three people, many systems are possible. After a pitch is led, one climber will clean the pitch while the third person jumars a free-hanging rope (either before or after the bag is hauled, depending on system used). This sounds like such a casual business, but in fact, the fellow jumaring a free line, 3,000 feet off the ground, twirling out in open space, has more than once wished his parents had never met. I (J.L.) once climbed a wall with three men and insisted on doing all of the leading because I was privately terrified to jug that free line.

For a three-person team, it is usually most efficient to have the person who jumared the free-hanging rope start to lead the next pitch while the previous pitch is still being cleaned (this may require a slightly larger rack; more gear

1. Climber leads.

2., 3. Leader sets up belay, anchoring climbing rope for second to begin cleaning pitch. Meanwhile the leader begins to haul the bag.

4. The bag hauled, the pitch cleaned, the second now becomes the leader of the next pitch.

Hanging belay rope management

Bill Hatcher photo

can be sent up to the leader, however, as the previous pitch is cleaned). With this three-person, twin-rack method, two climbers are always at work, and a difficult wall can usually be climbed faster than with the standard team of two.

TRANSITIONS

Making the transition from cleaning a pitch to leading the next pitch is often the most awkward moment on any wall, especially when the belay is crowded. A well-rigged belay, with anchors spread out as much as possible, simplifies the affair. Efficiency is key while getting the gear re-racked, obtaining an unsnarled belay from your partner, and making the first few placements off the belay anchor.

Remember to take the trail line. The belayer should always ask: Haul line? Pulley?

ROPES AND MANAGEMENT

The "spaghetti management system," where everything is left to hang and tangle as it will, is not recommended. Instead, careful organization and separation of the various ropes will save time and energy every time. Different colored ropes allow for quick identification. Stacking a rope through a sling keeps it from blowing around and getting snarled, as does using a rope bucket. Stacking the lead line and the haul line, and letting the lower-out line hang (single strand) is usually acceptable unless it's really windy; then all ropes should be stacked. If the haul line is left to hang, however, it's nice to clip it loosely to the belay with a Munter hitch or round robin, so that the leader doesn't have to deal with the full weight of the haul rope (give slack as needed).

Sometimes the leader will need additional gear sent up from the belay. He'll haul it up on the free-hanging haul line. This is simple if less than half the rope is out; if more than half is out, an additional line must be attached to the end of the haul line. Two solutions: 1) When leading, make sure that you have everything needed to finish the pitch as you near the half-rope point, or 2) unclip the haul line from the bags and tie in the lower-out line.

On the harder routes, I'll (J. M.) trail a 7-millimeter "zip line" (a fourth rope) instead of a haul line. Besides being lighter, gear can be sent up easily at any point on the pitch. At the end of the pitch, the zip line is then used to pull the haul line up.

FIXING PITCHES

It's standard practice to "fix" pitches on a long route prior to the final push to the summit. The team climbs as usual, cleaning most anchors, but leaving the rope in place after climbing each pitch. The team then descends and takes a rest (usually overnight); the fixed lines are then jumared and the climb continued. Most teams opt to fix the first two or three pitches, so on the next day some real altitude is gained before the bivy. For shorter walls (eight to twelve pitches), several ropes can be fixed so that the route can be done in a day from the ground. (It's quicker to jumar the fixed ropes in the early hours of the day than to lead those pitches.)

When fixing, fix "station to station," anchoring each rope into each belay. This enables the second jumarer to begin as soon as the first jumarer has passed the first anchor. The other method is to tie all the ropes together and shoot for the ground. On the steep side of El Cap (right side), this method is preferred because it eliminates all the potential edges that the rope would run over after each belay. This technique requires the ability to rappel past a knot, which is a specialized, complicated technique. It is most easily and safely accomplished like this: 1. Rappel down close to the knot (but not too close; some slack is needed to allow the weight to be taken on the ascender). 2. Clip in one or both of the jumars, attached to the waist with a daisy, and hang off the daisy. For safety, tie a backup knot a few feet below the knot connecting the ropes together, making sure to leave enough room to clip in your rappel device below the knot. Clip this backup knot into your harness before unclipping any jumars. 3. Allow slack to pass through the rappel device so all weight is suspended from the daisy. 4. Detach the rappel device, and reattach it below the knot. (Undo the backup knot that goes to your harness.) 5. Down-jumar with both jumar/daisy/aider sets until the rope is feeding through the rappel device. 6. Hold the rappel brake solid, unclip the ascenders from the rope, and continue rappelling.

Note: for safety when rapelling, keep one ascender connected via a daisy to the harness. If you were knocked unconscious by a falling rock, for example, the ascender would lock you off.

Free-hanging jumaring can be made less strenuous with the "Texas style" system: clip the top jumar into a daisy and through a chest harness (which can be rigged in the field with slings), and have both feet in two separate aiders (both feet in third step works well) on the bottom jumar.

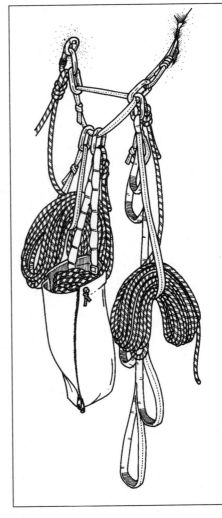

Rope stacking methods, (left to right:)

rope stacked in sling, A5 rope bucket, rope stacked in aider

The perils of fixed lines are considerable, evidenced by the many people who have died on them. Fixing lines, and the jumaring and rappelling to ascend and descend them, can (and often will) invite a mine field of potential problems, most of them potentially fatal. It is absolutely essential that you understand what can go wrong, so you can avoid mistakes, miscalculations, and oversights that can hurt you quickly and seriously. Almost anything that goes wrong on a fixed line is a disaster, so if you remember nothing else in this entire manual, remember the following.

Working on fixed lines is potentially hazardous because you are stressing both equipment and systems whose immediate status you can rarely verify by sight. For instance, if freak rockfall has all but severed one of the lines, it is virtually impossible to know so before the rope fails. You cannot see a nick in the rope 100 feet above you, and if the rope goes, so do you. Consider investing in some static lines if you plan on fixing a lot of ropes. Static lines are remarkably durable, many times more than a leading rope; and they can also double as haul lines.

Remember to anchor fixed lines when leaving them overnight; a stiff wind can blow them up and over a flake, rendering them irretrievable from below. The amount of tension while anchoring fixed lines is critical: too little, and a wind may blow them around a flake. More dangerous is too much tension. A wind can cause overly-tensioned ropes to saw through. Remember that after a rappel on a fixed line, the rope is stretched, and if you tie the rope in with any tension, expect a bowstring the next day because in the ensuing hours the rope will have shrunk back to its normal length. I've (J. M.) seen carabiners explode from a tightly tensioned fixed line, which then got wet, shrank, and blew out the anchor. On Mt. Hooker, I once had to jumar a 200-foot crusty, shredded line with only bits of sheath left. We'd left the line too tensioned the year before, and the oversight gave me the most frightening twenty minutes of my life.

Another factor is that lead ropes (not static lines) stretch when you jumar them, and if the line is running over even the slightest burr, the sawing action of several eager climbers jugging up can abrade the rope in half. I (J.L.) lost a friend on the Tangerine Trip, El Capitan, this way. So always be extremely vigilant about how you rig a fixed line. Nothing should be running over even the slightest edge; doublecheck everything before and after each rope switch; if you feel uncomfortable jumaring a fixed line, consider placing a prusik or Gibbs ascender above your ascenders. As you move up, your top jumar pushes the prusik or Gibbs along; if both jugs somehow pop off the line, the prusik or Gibbs will not. But this will not save you if the ropes have been hazardously rigged, or if an act of God has somehow damaged the lines. It's always a bit of a crap shoot with fixed ropes, no matter what you do.

*John Middendorf
jumaring fixed lines on
Zenyatta Mendatta, El
Capitan.*

John Middendorf collection
photo

Hauling

Far and away the most strenuous job on the wall is hauling the bags. Especially early on, when the water bottles are topped off and the food sacks are full, it often seems that moving all that freight up the wall is the very point of the climb. And when the bags snag on every little knob, the whole business can be cruel and hateful. The frustration factor is well-illustrated by an ascent of Half Dome I (J.L.) made with Mari Gingery and Janet Wilts. Just after the Thank God Ledge pitch, when I could almost spit to the summit, the bag hung up on a brow perhaps fifty feet below us. I yanked and fiddled and could not free it. Riled, I really put my back into it and managed to rip the grommets clean off the top of the bag, which whistled into the void. Had I taken ten minutes to rappel down and free it (which sometime you will have to do), I would have saved myself a whole day hiking back up to the base to recover the blasted bag. (Half of the contents were never found.)

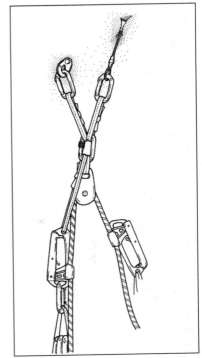

The basic haul system takes a few minutes to set up properly and requires a pulley and two ascenders. A sturdy, smooth-running pulley is essential (always bring a spare, too.) First, from your belay anchor matrix, pick a suitable placement to haul from. Hauling puts substantial stress on the anchor, so make sure it's one of the more substantial pieces in the belay matrix – one not given to shifting. Equalize two anchors if possible. Instead of connecting the pulley directly to a piece, use a sling to allow the pulley to rotate, thus reducing torque on the bearing. Also be aware that once you've hauled them up, you'll need to clip the bags off somewhere, so the haul point should be close to where you'll moor the bags. It's best to anchor the bags off to the side from where the team will hang, usually shoulder to shoulder, to reorganize for the next lead.

The basic hauling system

First, run the haul line through the pulley and clip the pulley in to the haul point. Next, set the anchoring ascender, clipping it upside down into the main haul anchor, then clamping it to the haul line leading directly to the haulbag below. By positioning it upside down, the line can be hauled up through it, but the cam on the ascender locks onto the rope at the end of each "pull" stroke. Some weight must be clipped into the bottom part of the upside down ascender to prevent it from lifting as the rope moves through it. Using a small rack for weight is the standard trick (clip it off with a

(opposite page)
Hauling from jumars
Bill Hatcher photo

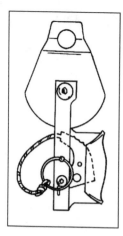

Rock Exotica's Wall Hauler.

locking biner so you don't lose the works). Then clip the other ascender, right side up, onto the rope just below the pulley, and you're set to haul. (In-depth pulling methods are discussed below.)

Self-camming hauling pulleys are now available, such as Rock Exotica's "Wall Hauler." These are incredibly convenient devices, avoiding the need to rig a jumar into each haul system. If you plan to do a lot of walls, buy one.

Before you can haul, the belayer must first free the bags from his anchor. On straight-up pitches, this is straightforward work. The leader hauls the slack out of the line, then a few feet more – or till the bag's considerable weight is off the bottom anchor – then the follower unclips the bags from the anchor. The standard signals are for the hauler to yell down that she's "ready to haul." Once she (the leader) has hauled the slack out of the system, the second unclips the bags and yells "haul away." It's not as important that you use these specific signals as it is to stay in communication with each other about what is being done – no matter how you phrase it. A standard set of signals is nice when communication is difficult or impossible – when it's windy, or the leader is around the corner. Generally, once the slack is hauled out and the haul line comes taut against the bag, the leader is – or should be – ready to haul, and the second is free to cut the bags loose. In places where you can't see or hear each other, it should be agreed in advance that when the haul line comes tight, the hauler has the system already set up and is ready to go. Cutting the bags loose prematurely is trouble, for it can shock-load the higher anchor and do all kinds of damage if the line is running around the leader's limbs.

On traversing pitches, it may be impossible for the leader to haul the bags off the lower anchor from the anchor above, because of the oblique angle of pull. Picture it: if the lead goes sideways, so does the haul line, and no matter how hard you yank on it, you're still pulling the bags, not up, but sideways. Assuming the bags are too heavy to lift by hand (and they often are), the simplest method is for the bottom climber to clip the lower-out line (tied into the haulbags) through a higher anchor, and minihaul the bags (with a belay device locked off) until their weight is off their anchor. Then, unclip the bags from the anchor and lower them out for the leader/hauler to have at it. Once the bags reach the higher anchor, you must clip them into the anchor. The process is

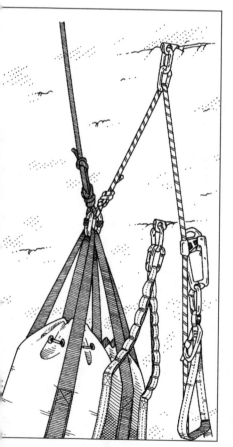

A mini-haul frees the haul bags from the anchor.

this: (1) Clip the haulbag daisy (a sling directly connected to the haulbags) into the anchor. (2) Lower the haulbags (reverse hauling) until their weight is no longer on the haul line. (3) Disassemble the haul system so that the pulley can be removed and readied for the next lead. (4) Clip in the haul rope short into the anchor as a direct back-up to the daisy. On numerous occasions, haulbags have come mysteriously unclipped, only to fall the full length of the rope. Bad news. It's amazing that such a shock load on the anchors have not cleaned teams right off the wall.

The favored big wall haul rope is a 200-foot, static, 9-millimeter line. The static lines do not stretch any appreciable length, which saves enormous amounts of energy. A normal lead line stretches so much that a large percentage of the energy put into hauling is absorbed by the dynamic qualities of the rope. Go with the static line. They are far better for fixing as well. Having the extra length of a 200-foot haul rope allows it to be used as an anchor line for rope-stretcher pitches (but it must be disassembled for the next pitch), and permits gear to be sent up to the leader (as a trail line) as far as 100 feet out.

Attached to the haulbag is the lower-out line, which allows the bags to be slowly lowered out on traversing pitches. Many parties on the Nose, for instance, who have only two ropes (lead and haul line – no lower-out line), simply cut their bags loose on one of several long traversing pitches (such as the pendulum pitch into the Stove Legs Cracks). This is not recommended; if the bag is poorly packed, the rough action of the bag bounding across the face can explode water bottles and force a team to retreat.

While cleaning, the follower should keep the lower out line connected to herself. A few good yanks can free the haulbag from snags. Expect the haulbag to hang up a couple of times on anything but entirely overhanging routes. Both the hauler and the cleaner should be aware of possible snags and be ready to deal with them. It's principally the cleaner's responsibility to free the hung bags, but there is a lot the hauler can do as well, especially if he is body-hauling with a long leash. Gently bouncing the bags up and down from the hauling station will free most bags; otherwise, lower the bags a few feet and try again. If this doesn't work, a yank from below on the lower-out line will usually do the job. If not, the cleaner will have to down-jumar and swing over to the stuck bags and free them.

If there is any chance of the bags knocking off loose rocks, make sure the cleaner is above the bags at all times. If there is considerable loose rock on the pitch, haul the bags after the pitch has been cleaned and the second is at the top belay station. Someone will have to descend to free the bags if they get hung up, but that's better than getting torpedoed by loose rocks.

Lowering out the bag

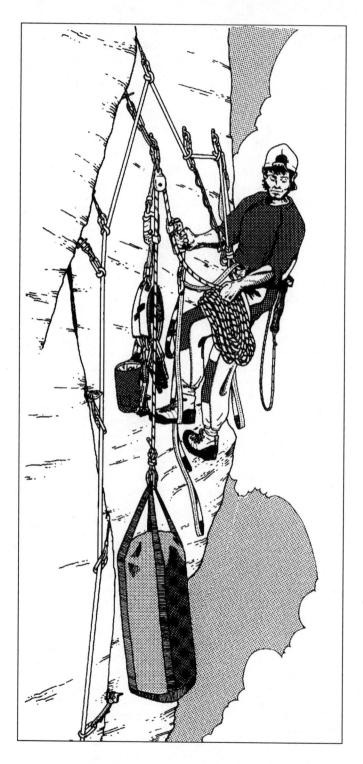

Leg-hauling a light load

HAULING METHODS

For light loads, leg-hauling is usually preferred. An aider is clipped into the hauling ascender, and the climber hauls by pumping a leg. For heavier loads (or when you're hauling from a ledge and the haul line is running over an edge, and the rope drag is brutal), go with the body-haul. The hauling ascender is clipped directly to the climber's harness, and full body weight is applied. Sometimes you may want to simultaneously heave directly on the rope with a gloved hand or another ascender. Body-hauling can be done in single stokes with the climber standing in aiders at the belay, allowing the climber to stay tied into the lead rope.

Xaver Bongard hanging out with the ravens on Great Trango Tower, Pakistan

John Middendorf photo

Longer length body-hauling is possible, lowering many feet at a time (up to a full rope length) as the bags are raised, and then jumaring back up. Here, your body acts as a counterweight against the bags. This "space hauling" may require untying from the lead line, so always tie into the extra rope from the haul line, backed up to the main anchor. Pulleys *have* broken (although very rarely), so back up the pulley with a sling and biner clipped loosely through the rope.

Since all loads get lighter the higher you climb (unless the team refuses food and drink), at some point the bags will be too heavy to leg haul and not quite heavy enough to want to rig the more complicated body-hauling system (requiring more slack and loops and tie-ins). Here, instead of straight leg-hauling, you weight the aider connected to the hauling jumar, and let your body weight, rather than your leg muscles, do the task. Much depends on how big or small a climber is.

Bags hang free on El Capitan.

McDevitt photo

For loads over 200 pounds, two separate hauls are recommended. Simpler, however, is the two-person haul system. The cleaner somehow gets the bags off the anchor (with help from the leader/hauler), then cleans the pitch.

Body-hauling

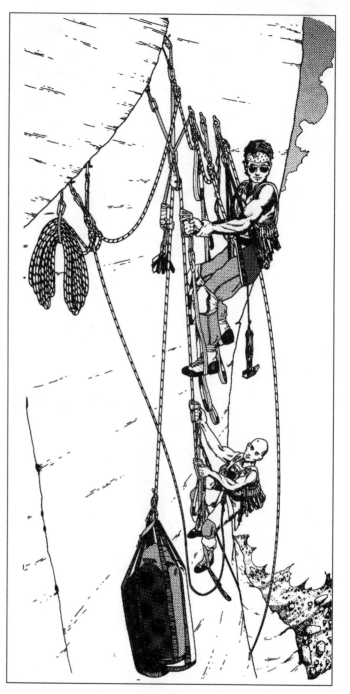

Counterweight hauling

He'll then act as a "dead weight," clipped on with his jumars to the other end of the haul line, while the leader hauls in the traditional manner. Again, make sure that the "dead weight" person is backed up with a belay rope.

These are the standard techniques. It's up to you to

determine the most efficient method at a given time. The need for continuous good communication cannot be overstated. Use the standard commands ("Ready to haul," "Haul away," etc.) and agree to make it understood that when the haul line comes tight, the belayer is free to cut the bags loose (in case you can't hear each other). Again, cutting the bags loose when the hauler is not quite ready is almost always big trouble.

Hauling Past Knots

When the wall is overhanging, you will sometimes fix two pitches with two ropes tied together. In this case, two pitches are hauled as one, which entails hauling the knot (which connects the two ropes together) through the system.

This is tricky business, usually requiring either hauling temporarily through a carabiner or lowering the hauling anchor. In short: haul until the knot is just below the anchoring ascender, which will hold the bags as the knot transfer is made. Two methods are now possible. For reasonably-sized loads, the bags can be hauled temporarily through a higher anchor (at least a foot above), and through a carabiner. With the knot now about 10 inches above the pulley, it should be possible to reassemble the pulley set-up with the knot on the other side of the pulley. Then continue.

If a higher anchor is unavailable, or if the loads are extreme and can't be hauled through a biner, it's possible to pass the knot by lowering the haul point. Again, haul until the knot is as high as possible, and temporarily tie the bags off with slings. Next, lengthen the tie-in to the anchoring ascender (usually done with slings). Suspend the pulley set-up from an appropriate-length sling until it can be reassembled with the knot on the other side. Note: with the "Wall Hauler," by Rock Exotica, a separate anchoring ascender must be set to allow a knot to be passed.

HAULBAGS

A good haulbag is essential. On my (J. M.) first big wall, the NW face of Half Dome, we used a canvas duffle bag with speedy-stitched straps running along the sides. After dragging it up twenty pitches, the bottom seam finally blew out and ejected all the contents just as we reached the rim. The next day we spent ten hours combing through the manzanita below, and only recovered half our gear.

The A5 and Fish white vinyl haulbags are the most durable. When making or buying a big wall haulbag, make sure the material is both strong and abrasion resistant (these

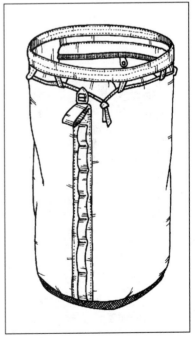

A5 Haulpack

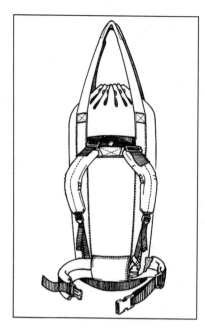

Big Wall Haulbag with detachable shoulder straps

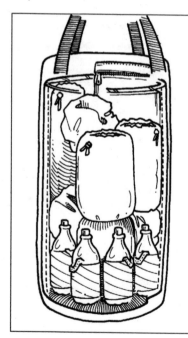

A well-packed haulbag (stuff extra space with soft goods: jackets, etcetera.

do not always go hand-in-hand). Padded carrying straps are required for long approaches. Stout, wide haulbags are far easier to get in and out of (and pack) than long, sausage-shaped articles. Offset haul straps allow one set of straps to be detached from the haul point for easier access inside.

Packing the Haulbag

Just as with packing for any trip, the haulbag always seems too small at first. The trick is to lay out all the items deemed essential for the trip (discarding a few in the process), then coming up with a general packing plan. It pays to have the bag properly organized. Certain things (like storm gear) need to be more accessible than other items (like reserve food and water). Make sure water bottles, especially on lower angle routes, are well-padded.

Any bulge (beware of cans) will quickly turn into a hole no matter the fabric of the bag. Minimize damage by creating a smooth cylinder. A foam sleeping pad is the first item to go into a haulbag. Next, pile in those items you won't need for the initial few days. If the wall is longer than three days, pack the food into two bags: one for the initial half of the route, and one for the final half. The final days food bag goes into the bottom, along with the bulk of the water, making sure everything is surrounded and protected by the foam pad. Next, pack a storm item (a bivouac sack or rain pants) to pad around the bottom of the haulbag. Then check the bottom, from the outside, to ensure that all the bottom space is completely filled. If not, use more clothing to shim up the bottom.

The crux of packing is now over. The remaining space is filled with more storm gear (generally not in stuff bags, so clothes can be packed around other items), sleeping bags, the other food bag, jackets, miscellaneous items, and some water for the day.

A few more tips: Having a pocket in the top of the haulbag makes organization simpler. Lots of stuff sacks are required for good organization. Make sure each stuff sack has a full-strength clip-in loop (for clipping in when reorganizing the haulbag on the wall). Also, in wet weather, pack the sleeping bag first, in a heavy-duty, waterproof garbage bag, then stuff it into a stuff sack.

Connecting Haulbags to the Haul Line

The haul line must be detachable from the haulbags (clip the haul line into the haulbags with either two opposing biners or a jumbo locking biner). Protect the knot in the haul rope with a few wraps of tape, or (better) cover the knot with the cut-off top of a water bottle. If you don't, the constant abrasion of the knot against the rock will grind the sheath right off, in as little as one pitch.

Big nailups require big loads, so two or more haulbags are often necessary – as well as portaledge haulbags, and perhaps a smaller pack. Multiple haulbags must be connected so they can be daisied off to an anchor, while still allowing access to each haulbag. Using a separate "haul cord" facilitates linking two haulbags together.

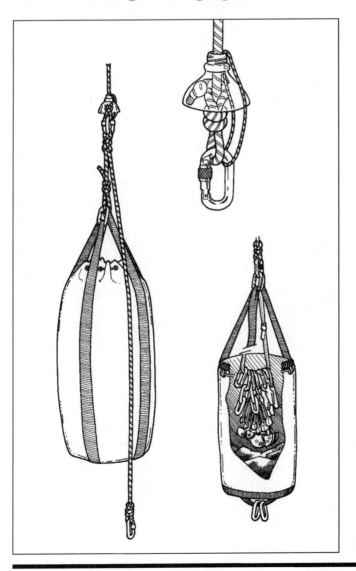

Climbers on Lunar Ecstacy, Zion National Park.

Bill Hatcher photo

A haul cord is fashioned from at least ten feet of sturdy 9-millimeter cord. Tie the haul cord directly into one of the two straps of each haulbag, then tie a figure eight knot in between. With this knot, the haul line will be attached with two opposed carabiners. The other straps are secured with a biner connected to the haul cord. One end of the haul cord can be extra long to allow one bag to hang below the other bag. A daisy, used to secure the bags at each belay, is girth hitched to the figure eight knot. The portaledge haul sacks can then be clipped into the straps of the haulbag. As with all of these descriptions, the only sure way to understand everything is to re-read them after studying the attending illustration.

Multi-day Routes

Multi-day big walls (Grade V – overnight, and Grade VI – two or more days) require far more gear than single-day routes, so weight becomes a primary factor. Every piton and nut should be cherry-picked for optimal function, based on weight and bulk. Bring too much, and your trip becomes a hauling job from hell; too little, and the ascent (and your life) may be jeopardized. Since weight is so crucial, spare gear is virtually never hauled up a wall. So whatever gear you do bring must be in good condition and up for the task. You'll use every piece of gear over and over, beating on it with a hammer, yanking on it, falling on it, cursing at it. If the gear isn't sound to begin with, get set to cry a river when it breaks – because it will.

Loaded for El Cap.
Bill Hatcher photo

First, pick your partner. We've touched on this already, but a few other thoughts are worthwhile. Before tackling a serious, week-long wall, the team should have already weathered a few epics together on shorter routes. This tends to either temper or atomize the combined personalities. Character is transformed (sometimes radically) by the high crag, so don't assume that a close friend will make an suitable partner. We're talking about a person's basic stuff here, and more than once I've seen a perfect Solomon regress into a regular Mr. Hyde by the second bivouac. Best to get all that established on a short wall before casting off for a long one.

As for the route, start with a clean (hammerless) wall, where you can work out the procedural bugs where the level of complexity and commitment is comparatively lower. Study the topo carefully, and estimate the number of days for your ascent. This will determine the amount of food and water you'll need.

Once you've chosen a partner and a route, the next task is to gather the gear. Start with the rack. Basic racks have been covered previously, but perhaps the route has special requirements – for example, more thin pitons, or major wide gear for off-widths. Study the topo, and talk to anyone who has recently climbed the route for information on the suitable rack. Remember, routes change, so while someone who climbed the route ten years ago can give you global comments about location, exposure, ledges, free climbing scenarios, how to get off the wall once climbed, and so forth, the fitting rack will almost assuredly have changed over the years, owing to the aid cracks getting beaten out. Best to get the latest from someone who has just climbed the route. With a little searching, you can usually find him or her.

The normal procedure is to spread out a big tarp and lay out all of the rack according to sizes. You want to see all the gear, appraise the condition of each piece, discarding this, adding that. Cross-reference the topo and any other info you've gleaned from other climbers. Most likely you'll end up eliminating all but the most essential items, once you see the sheer bulk of what you have. Once you've finalized the selection, rack it up.

Next, organize all the rest: ropes, personal aid gear, bivouac and storm gear, and food and water. Decide whether you will fix the initial pitches of the climb, and plan the general strategy. Finally, pack all the gear in appropriate haulbags, and get psyched for a stint on the vertical.

BIVOUACS AND PORTALEDGES

Bivouacs can range from the best to the worst times of your life. Much depends on your psychological state, the prevailing conditions, and the vagaries of the rock where you're stuck for the night (are there good ledges, and so on). Much of this is beyond your control, so you focus on what you can control – namely, gear. As little as ten years ago, bivouacs were Spartan affairs. With the advent of new gear, principally the portaledge, most bivouacs have become something to really look forward to.

The first questions: Are there ledges to sleep on? And what will happen if it storms?

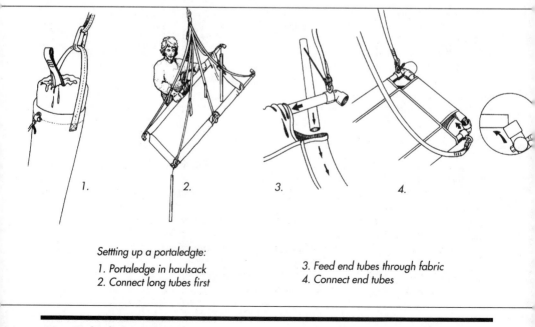

Settting up a portaledgte:
1. Portaledge in haulsack
2. Connect long tubes first

3. Feed end tubes through fabric
4. Connect end tubes

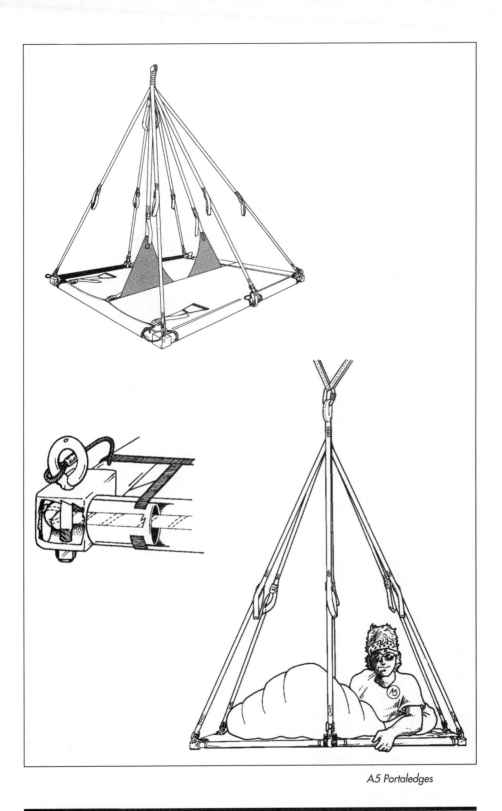

A5 Portaledges

Salathe Wall, El Capitan
Bill Hatcher photo

If there are no ledges, hammocks or portaledges are required. Before portaledges (specially-constructed hanging tents which are suspended from a single point), hammocks were usually used for long routes. Lightweight, but terribly uncomfortable, they were always a liability in stormy conditions. The difference between hammocks and portaledges is the difference between longing for first light so you can claw out of a straitjacket, and dreading first light because it means getting out of bed and back to work. Portaledges have, in fact, revolutionized big wall climbing, and have become required gear for multi-day routes requiring hanging bivouacs.

Portaledges are available in both single and double models. Single ledges offer far more personal space; doubles sleep two and save weight. The A5 double portaledge has offset "sharkfin" dividers down the middle of the ledge. This gives maximum room for sleeping head to toe, while dividing the space comfortably. Single ledges come in two basic styles of suspension: four-point and six-point. Four-point suspensions are lighter and less prone to tangles. They also double as a comfortable chair, with your legs hanging out the middle outside of the ledge. For structural reasons, double portaledges require six-point suspension. If you're planning to do most of your walls in accessible areas, like Yosemite, the single ledge is the way to go; for remote areas, where every ounce is crucial, double portaledges are the choice (they're also warmer, allow for team cooking, and so on). Currently, only two manufacturers make portaledges: A5 Adventures and Fish Products. Both brands are excellent wall vehicles.

A heavy-duty, seam-sealed rainfly is essential. In general, always expect a storm, and be well-practiced in setting up the whole system from a hanging station. Setting up in windy conditions requires having the set-up wired.

Always stay tied in at the bivouac. For the night I'll sometimes replace my harness with a small supertape sling harness. It's nice to have a free end of the rope to tie into, with a lot of slack. Ascenders attached to this allow for fine adjustments and moving around.

EXTENDED BELAYS

For long, arduous routes, where each lead may require three or more hours, belaying on the portaledge makes for luxurious belays. On steep terrain, when it's not too windy, the portaledge can be hauled rigid. Alternatively, a comfortable seat can be fashioned out of wood or sheet aluminum – a sort of bos'n's chair. About two feet square and padded, it has two holes drilled in the corners, and one in the center. Rig with slings (the center sling should be adjustable). Otherwise, a belay seat is advised. You don't want to be hanging off your harness for hours at a time.

FOOD AND WATER FOR GRADE VIs

Food and water comprise much of the weight on multi-day climbs. The rule of thumb is ½ gallon (approximately two liters) per person per day. Water weighs 8.2 pounds per gallon. This is a minimal ration, and requires conservation. Food weighs about three pounds per person per day (with canned food as the staple). Total provisions for a team of two per day equals 14.2 pounds. Total for a five-day wall: 71 pounds. Quite a load, but it lessens with the ascent. Try to scrimp on either food or water and learn to hate life.

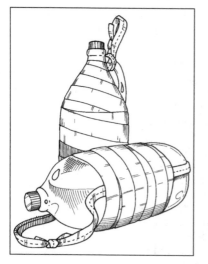

Water bottles, taped for durability

Food is a matter of preference, of course. For a five-day wall in Yosemite, I'll (J. M.) typically take five or six cans of dinners (cans are good because of their water content), three or four cans of fruit, a box of granola to mix in with the fruit for breakfast, four half-dozen packages of bagels and cream cheese, single packages of condiments for the bagels, a couple packages of Fig Neutrons, and a selection of candy bars (make sure to get the sealed wrapper type for use in hot weather). Some hard candies (like Jolly Rancher's) are also good to keep your mind off the water while hanging around belays. Energy bars are excellent because the action is from dawn to dusk without much time for extended lunch breaks. The drawback is that without sufficient water to wash them down, your throat might feel likes it's full of quick set cement.

For water, two-liter plastic soda bottles are the standard (they're nearly impossible to break, or even blow the top off – try it). Water bottles get abused while in the haul-bag. Flimsy ones make themselves known as you desperately watch a wet spot grow on the side of the haulbag. Make sure to have a clip-in loop on all water bottles (duct-tape a sling around the bottle). Bring at least ½ gallon per person per day (survival rations), and twice that for hot weather. On my (J. M.) first time up the Nose route (circa 1980, 100 degrees), I miscalculated water needs and spent two days without it. I learned my lesson about conserving and rationing water for a climb. On the last day of a new wall on Mt. Watkins (in mid-August), I (J.L.) drank two gallons of water in one hour.

Luxury food items include perishable vegetables, tortillas, and the like. A five-gallon painter's bucket, rigged with slings, makes a great haulable container. Hook underneath the haulbag. Also, a stove is excellent – for coffee in the morning, and heating up the canned dinners. For alpine big walls, stoves are essential.

PERSONAL EQUIPMENT FOR GRADE VIs

Sleeping Bags and Foam Pads

Synthetic insulation is the way to go. In storms, it's impossible to stay completely dry, due to the water pouring off the wall. A clip-in loop sewed on is essential on your sleeping bag. Don't do what Eric Kohl did on our (J.M.) first ascent, Route 66, on Yosemite Falls Wall. In lieu of a clip-in loop, he secured his bag with the draw cord while he down-jumared to retrieve more beer from the haulbag. It was a windy night. The draw cord blew out and for the next few nights his teeth sounded like a pair of those wind-up dentures you buy in a joke store. But it was no joke to Eric.

A good foam sleeping mat is basic wall gear. Used to pad the haulbag during the day, a foam pad is invaluable on cold nights, where a bottom insulating layer is required. Avoid the thick ground pads – they take up too much space in the haulbag. "Karrimats" are the best.

Storm Gear and Extra (warm) Clothing

Always be prepared for fierce weather. On my (J.L.) first few Yosemite walls, my bivouac equipment consisted of a wool blanket and a balaclava. No sleeping pad, even. Of course, summer nights in Yosemite are usually mild, but not always. I've seen temperatures exceed 90 degrees one day, followed by a horrendous storm that cloaked the top three hundred feet of El Capitan in a sheet of ice one foot thick. During one such storm, a Japanese team got caught on the last hanging belay on the Nose and perished, still tied into the bolts and entombed in two feet of ice.

During thunderstorms, water collects as it washes down the wall, and a regular flash flood can start pouring down the face in minutes. Good protection includes a rain jacket, rain pants or bibs, and a bivouac sack. Warm gloves are a must for moving in cold and stormy weather. When cold fingers become inoperable, it's really dangerous. Bring an extra hat and gloves, in addition to a full (top and bottom) polypro underlayer. In a storm, shed all cotton and clothe more appropriately.

I've (J. M.) been in more storms on big walls than I can count, and for certain, those epics were some of the most frightening and miserable times of my life. In 1986, I was rescued off the South Face of Half Dome in a brilliant helicopter rescue which swooped in and plucked us off in between storm fronts. We were totally trapped by the storm for three hellish days and nights. Without the rescue, we were goners. I've likewise been caught in bad storms on El Cap, amazed by how ferocious Mother Nature can strike in the comparatively genteel area of Yosemite Valley. Even with state-of-the-art storm gear, Jimmy Dunn and I suffered miserably on an ascent of Cosmos, principally due to our exposed position when the storm hit. We shivered convulsively for three days and three sleepless nights as we battled our way up the final pitches in bleak weather.

Some routes require more extensive storm gear. When Mugs Stump and I (J.M.) did the first winter ascent of the Hallucinogen Wall in the Black Canyon, we wore full expedition clothing. Though the weather held, a bad storm could have trapped us severely, with no chance of rescue (in winter, it is a major alpine climb/descent just getting to the start of the climb). The point is, you can never beat the storm. The most you can do is tie it, and survive. In a really grim contest, your life depends on your gear.

Harnesses

All commercially available wall harness are stronger than you'll ever need, meaning you cannot come ripping out of them and go windmilling into the void – no matter how long a fall you might take. Given this, and since you'll be hanging in your harness for the better part of each day, the first consideration is fit and comfort. Pick one with a wide (three- to four-inch) waist harness and well-padded leg loops. Next, make sure the unit is constructed to suspend you close to the waist. This is accomplished with separate leg loops, allowing you to tie the rope through both the leg loops and the waist harness. This style of harness also accepts a belay/rappel loop (a strong three-inch loop of one-inch sewn webbing), which is key for comfortable hanging on the vertical. Other key design concepts are strong gear loops, a full strength clip-in loop on the back of the harness – for clipping on the trail line – and detachable leg loops (for dumps) that can be dropped while still allowing the climber to remain tied in.

Shoes

Any medium-weight hiking boot will do for big wall climbing. A reasonably stiff sole is desired, since you'll be standing in aiders for hours at a time. Jumaring is hell on the toe area, so look for a pair with a durable rand around the toe. Optimum wall boots are comfortable for both hiking and standing in aiders, yet allow for a reasonably high standard of free climbing. The best option is to resole a tight-fitting, durable, medium-weight pair of high-top boots with climbing rubber. For extended free climbing, a comfortable pair of free-climbing shoes should be brought along: make sure that they are comfy enough for long stretches of climbing, and possibly some hanging in aiders (no slippers or tight boots). Clip-in loops of parachute cord, strung through an eyelet, are nice for clipping in your shoes at night. Drop your only shoes, kiss your feet goodbye. It's happened, and the survivors walk with a cane to this day.

Kneepads

Knees get battered on walls, especially while hauling close to a belay, so a pair of kneepads is vital. A light, soft and flexible pair, available at most sport shops, works fine.

Gloves

Cleaning and hauling will trash your hands, so a pair of fingerless gloves are a must. Thin, durable, tight-fitting (goatskin leather is best) gloves like the "Trucker's Special," widely available at hardware stores, are the ticket. Cut off the fingers above or below the middle knuckle, depending on how accurate you are with your hammer. Understand that wounds will not properly heal on a wall, no matter how long you're on one. There's too much grime involved. So protective measures are needed. Some climbers go with tape. Go with the gloves.

Headlamps

Each climber needs a headlamp for tasks at night – like finishing a pitch, or setting up the bivy. First choice is the Petzl Zoom, which fits securely on your head without a separate battery pack and the attending cable. For cold weather, the Petzl Arctic head lamp, with a chest-mounted battery pack, is useful. Bring extra bulbs and batteries, and test your headlamps prior to starting the wall. When Mike Corbett and I (J. M.) attempted the first one-day ascent of the Shield, we made it to Chickenhead Ledge (three pitches from the top) in seventeen hours, only to find (at dusk) that we only had one working headlamp. During the ensuing forced bivy, a storm blew in at midnight, and with only t-shirts and cotton pants, we suffered mightily. Go prepared.

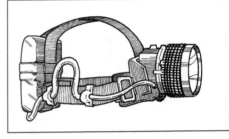

Petzl Arctic headlamp

The issue of batteries is still an open debate. Various kinds of lithium batteries are available, and they normally last far longer than the normal unit. (They also cost about six times as much). The problem is that there is no simple way to verify just how much juice these batteries have. Many new lithium batteries will keep a head lamp lit or eight hours or more. However, on a caving expedition in Venezuela, I (J.L.) had two "new" lithiums go dead after only a few hours, and was left to claw my way out of a nasty cavern (over seven miles) with a Bic lighter and the faint glow of a cheap cigar. Whatever kind of battery you go with, bring plenty of backups.

MISCELLANEOUS WIDGETS FOR GRADE VIs

Stuff sacks of various sizes, with sewn clip-in loops, are required for organizing food and bivy gear. Rarely can you set things down to reorganize, as you do on the ground. Bring a small repair kit and a suitable first aid kit. The repair kit should include duct tape, a sewing awl for fabric repairs, and a small can of WD-40 for camming units after they get wet in a storm. The first aid kit should include some cloth tape and antibiotic ointment for cuts and abrasions, aspirin for morning hand cramp, and other basic items. And bring a can opener (best: a Swiss army knife) and a spoon. Anything that will be moved around (jackets, stuffbags, water bottles, etc.) requires a clip-in loop.

Tape decks/radios are optional, but for big routes involving long hours docked at a belay, tunes are a welcome companion. The intensity of a belay is made so by the long silences. Most climbers find it refreshing to break things up with an occasional tape or radio broadcast; most who think they feel otherwise have yet to spend ten days on a bleak wall. But tastes differ.

I'll (J. M.) usually bring a book and some candles (to save head lamp use) for some night reading – to lull me to sleep. And I always aid climb with a low-profile hip pack (allowing chimneying with it on), containing essential everyday items like a Swiss army knife and cloth tape.

BOLTING GEAR

A small bolt kit is required gear for any route of medium difficulty on up. Uses include replacing bad belay bolts, setting bivouac rivets, or drilling emergency anchors for retreating. A couple of ¼-inch drills, a drill holder, drift pin, and a few ¼-inch bolts with hangers should be ample. (Note: Some routes, such as Never-Never Land, El Cap, have hangerless bolts at the belays. In such cases, bring five or six hangers.) Also include some ¼-inch coarse-thread nuts and a wrench for the occasional nutless thread-head Rawldrive. On established routes, you should never need the bolt kit. If you start drilling on lead where others did not, you're in over your head, and should retreat.

The bolt kit is an emergency backup, and should always be considered as such. However, winter rockfall, for example, can shear away crucial bolts, and if you have no gear to replace them, you're in a bad way.

RETREATING

Retreating off big walls is often serious business. When you add 200-pound haulbags and free-hanging rappels into the equation, it can get downright dangerous – and terrifying. Especially difficult are descents off routes that overhang (in whole or part); down-nailing is often required. Once you've reached the halfway point on a wall, most climbers feel that "the only way off is up." There's a shade of macho posturing in this credo, but with so much steep rock already below you, and in light of all the mid-air dangling, anchor switches, rappelling, bag lowering, and lost gear involved in reversing directions, it's almost always easier to carry on. Retreating from trade routes is normally an easier affair, however, because so many parties have changed their minds along the route, and fixed rappel stations are often in place most (if not all) the way down. Still, there are risks, and retreat should only be considered when finishing the climb is tangibly more hazardous than the real and many dangers of bailing off it.

To safeguard against retreat, pick a good time to start the route, watching for danger signs like cirrus clouds (though pioneer wall climber Charlie Porter once said, "If you wait for the weather, you'll never do jack-shit"). Predict and prepare for all eventualities. Consider emergency strategies at every stage of the route – what will you do if a partner gets injured, for example. Mull various scenarios and how you would resolve them. Weather can be a devil. Proper storm gear will often prevent an emergency retreat. Minimum heavy weather gear for non-portaledge routes like the Nose includes a tube tent and a bivy sack. For anything else, come prepared for the worst, because you might get it.

Self-rescue is the preferred escape. Calling for a rescue should be avoided unless absolutely necessary. Understand that a rescue is always an involved business, with serious dangers for your rescuers. When a storm hits, it's often better to batten down for a day or two, rather than trying to ascend or descend when soaking wet – which increases the chances of getting hypothermia, a common and life-threatening condition when you're cold and wet. Remember that outside the boundaries of National Parks, rescues are unlikely. For most walls, self-rescue is it.

That much said, appreciate that no climber's success ratio is 100%, or anything close to it. There are too many things that can go wrong, many of them psychological. I (J.L.) remember the first time I tried to climb El Capitan, when I was seventeen. Hauling the bag on top of the Half Dollar, perhaps 1,000 feet up the Salathé Wall, I heard a terrific racket off to the side, glanced over and saw a body cartwheeling down the great prow of the Nose. There was no mistaking what I saw, and the stupendous noise – as if God had grabbed the air and was tearing it in half – combined with the chilling image of the climber plummeting down the cliff at terminal velocity, dashed my resolve to climb El Cap, or to climb at all. An extreme case, granted, but things happen, and if you don't feel like climbing, it's probably better to bail off low down, rather than pushing on and hating life up higher. Though wall climbing goes beyond fun in almost all directions, the venture has to have an aspect of pleasure to it – no matter how small – lest the whole thing turns into an exercise for zealots and fanatics. As they say, go when your mind is right. And don't expect it always will be.

Rappelling with a haulbag.

DESCENT

Some walls have walk-offs; others, rappels off the flanks of the formation; still others (though rarely, such as desert spires/towers) require rappelling the entire climbing route. Descending with gear is best facilitated by hanging the haulbag from the harness, though massive bags must be lowered independently. On circuitous routes, the bags must be tethered and reeled in to the lower anchor/belay.

WASTE AND GARBAGE

The first question most non-climbers ask is: "How do you, you know, relieve yourself up there?" Standard answer: drop your drawers and go for it, same as on the ground. If there's no one below, most climbers hang it out in space, since bags full of excrement littering the base of a cliff are long-lasting and repulsive. On routes with people below, common courtesy is to do your business in some sort of container, and toss it far from the wall. Never defecate into a crack – it's disgusting, and smells horribly for months afterward. In fact, everything about the "standard" methods is disgusting and irresponsible from any kind of ecological and aesthetic perspective. But that's the way the first wall climbers did it, and in actual practice, that's how 99% of all climbers do it today.

When wall climbers numbered in the few dozens, the impact of human waste was negligible. But as wall climbing gains popularity, new thinking is in order. Given that on any summer day upwards of a dozen teams can normally be spotted on El Capitan, for instance, the old methods of simply letting it fly are no longer acceptable, and haven't been for years. As far back as 1975, I can remember that El Cap Spire (Salathé Wall) and Camp 6 (Nose) were regular latrines, with stench enough to buckle the knees of a cigar store Indian. Future regulations may require bringing all human waste up with you. If so, a three-inch diameter PVC pipe, with screwable end caps and packed with lime, may be a starting point. It's long overdue that new thinking be introduced, at least in the more traveled areas.

Trash (cans, wrappers, etc.), should always be carried up, since throwing garbage off routes is littering, plain and simple, even if you plan to return to pick it up (which is never successful in retrieving much). The base of El Cap and Half Dome, despite almost annual cleanup efforts, look more and more like city dumps with each passing year. So haul your trash. Always. Most cans can be flattened with hammers, and paper waste can be stuffed into a stuff sack for that purpose.

BAG THROWING

Throwing haulbags off the top of the wall is illegal in National Parks; if caught doing so, you'll be charged with "creating a hazardous situation." In an area where you can throw bags off the top, you can either chuck a bag with only soft stuff (sleeping bags, clothes, slings, etc.) or throw heavy stuff rigged with a parachute fashioned from aiders (for parachute cords) and portaledge rainflys (for the parachute). Never pitch anything breakable (cans, portaledges, camming units, biners), and tie hardware (pitons) together with a sling so if the bag blows out, the pins are together. Pad hardware with ensolite and sleeping bags. Heavy stuff will go near the bottom. Pack a sleeping bag at the top and tie the haulbag's opening loosely: the sleeping bag will blow out the top of the haulbag at impact, absorbing much of the shock (otherwise the haulbag will probably blow apart). If there is any chance of striking other people either on the wall or at the base, throwing bags is not an option.

I (J.L.) personally feel that jettisoning bags is an emergency measure – when a team is facing grim weather, or trying to evacuate an injured climber – and should never be employed to take the bite out of a strenuous descent. One thing's for sure: no matter how you pack the bags and regardless of the parachute device you rig, the bag will generally blow out at impact and the gear will take a thrashing. It may take you hours to locate it at the base. More than once, thieves have made off with the whole lot before the team was even off the cliff. For the majority of cases, the hassles of trying to find the pitched gear, plus the inevitable damage done to bags and equipment, far outweigh the grief of simply schlepping the loads down on your back. There are exceptions, of course, such as when you're descending steep terrain and racing against the sun. If it's a straight shot to the deck, it's always better to cut the bags loose rather than spend a night in slings.

Xaver Bongard soloing
Jolly Roger, El Capitan.

Bill Hatcher photo

CHAPTER 10

Advanced Aid Techniques

Now that big wall systems are behind us, let's concentrate on the fine points of difficult aid pitches. To climb with any modicum of safety, extreme aid (new wave ratings of A3+ or harder) requires experience and judgement. On pitches rated A4 and above, the climbing is often dangerous, requiring acute concentration, patience, and time. Good testing methods (the bounce test) were discussed previously, and are essential for hard aid. Remember to always stay low while testing a marginal piece, and consider the forces involved on the piece you are on if the tested piece pulls. Ideally, the lower piece can withstand a sudden transfer of your weight if the tested placement blows – as it

Testing a poor piton placement.

often will on hard aid. Aggressive bounce testing, properly done, is the single most important technique that allows aid climbers to link together, with some measure of confidence, a string of marginal placements.

To describe difficult aid is to describe fear. Hard aid is commonly defined as looking at a serious fall on marginal protection. The dangers are not momentary; they span hours, even days. And the actual deed of moving up, from one placement to the next, constitutes only about one percent of the time spent on an arduous aid pitch. The rest is spent in figuring out the placement, setting it, and testing it. You'll be climbing on borderline placements, utterly committed because nothing is worthy of lowering off from, farther and farther removed from anything secure (and seemingly miles away from any upcoming security), testing subsequent placements less and less for fear of any sudden motion, panic and fear barely held in check, finally stepping on an untested tied-off knifeblade because the present hook placement just crumbled into nothingness, looking at a long, long fall, possibly with a ledge to hit below (when you're up there, measurement in feet is meaningless), and then watching the knifeblade shift suddenly, praying it will remain keyed in the crack.... Later, when you've arrived at a bomber piece, the entire experience (which may have lasted the better part of a day) is labeled simply as "hard" or "scary," or "A-whatever." Good fun, if you're up for it.

Hard aid consists of hooking, copperheading, thin nailing, and expanding placements. We'll look at each of these in turn.

Hooks of various kinds:

(top row, from left) Chouinard Standard, Chouinard Pointed, Leeper Flat, Leeper Pointed.

(bottom row, from left) Black Diamond Hook, Fish Hook, Homemade Ring Angle Claw

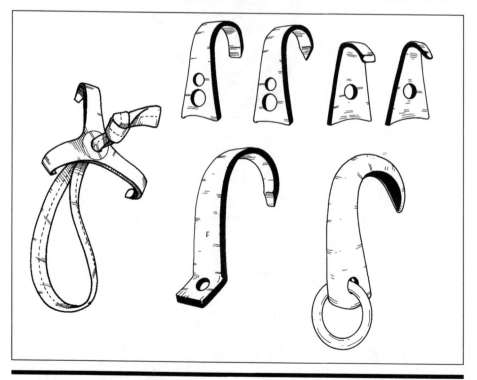

HOOKING

There are three basic types of hooks: the "Chouinard," the Leeper Logan (flat and pointed), and the ring-angle claw. The Chouinard hook is the classic, most commonly used hook. Even moderate nailing routes usually require two of them. As with all hooks, bring an extra in case one is dropped. For grim aid, "pointed Chouinards" are required (a standard Chouinard hook with the end filed into a sharp, 45-degree, triangular point). These are used in enhanced hook placements, where a shallow ¼-inch hole has been drilled in a horizontal or sloping shelf, allowing the hook to "catch."

The flat Leeper hooks are stable on certain narrow edges where a Chouinard would "rock" (very frightening). On thin, lower-angle aid, a filed flat-Leeper (where half of the hooking edge is filed off) can be useful. The pointed Leeper hooks have many uses, most notably for bat-hooking, an archaic technique developed by Warren Harding in which shallow ¼-inch holes are drilled in blank rock to provide hook placements. (Modern climbers will generally fill shallow holes with ⁵⁄₁₆-inch, coarse-thread machine head bolts, available for pennies at any hardware store.) Sometimes a slight tap sets the hook nicely while bathooking, but beware: if you pound them in, they are likely to spring out suddenly.

Ring-angle claws, the largest of the hook rack, derive their name from the old, soft iron pitons from which these previously hard-to-find hooks are fashioned. Years ago, you'd have to search desperately for a particular long, soft iron, ring-angle piton and bend it into the proper shape (this took some practice, moreover). Ring-angle claws are essentially an enlarged version of the regular hook. The Fish hook is the only commercially made large hook on the market. The best big hooks are those which are somewhat malleable for precision shaping per placement. Large hooks are essential on many routes, their uses ranging from hooking two-inch-thick detached flakes, to hooking a large solid shelf. For some routes, several sizes of large hooks may be required.

For an extreme aid route, the hook rack may consist of ten different hooks in a variety of sizes and shapes: three basic Chouinards, one regular Leeper flat, one modified Leeper flat, two Leeper pointeds, and three ring-angle claws of various sizes.

Sometimes hooks must be used to clean a hook lead. John Middendorf on the Wyoming Sheep Ranch, El Capitan.

John Middendorf Collection

Slinging Leeper Hooks

The Leeper Cam Hook in action.

Hooking Techniques

Familiarity with the various hooks and knowing when each one is best used is essential. Practice on the boulders (*not* the chalked ones, as hooks can sometimes blow out a small edge) to get a feeling for the work. When hooking, always keep a daisy connected to the hook/aider so it doesn't blow away or become lost during a fall. Hooking sounds scary, but many hook placements are bomber; some are so secure they can be left for protection, perhaps even duct-taped to the stone to secure them. Sometimes a slight tap with the hammer will set a hook securely on a flake. Not all hooks are secure, most notably when a hook is on a sloping edge and the hook can skate. When on a hook, keep your weight straight under it. Shifting side to side can cause the hook to rock and pop off. Long reaches to blind hook placements are frightening and not unheard of on bleak aid. Experiment low to the ground, and learn for yourself. Practice is the best (and really the only) instructor.

COPPERHEADING

Copperheads (or "mashheads") are cylinders of copper or aluminum swaged onto a cable; they are mashed into shallow grooves or pockets as aid placements. First created (in the early '70s) by Bill Forrest as a nut, climbers later discovered that they could be hammered into seams and made to stick.

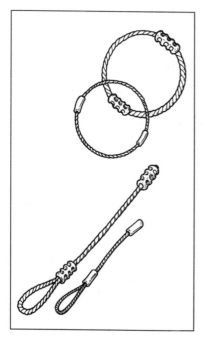

Circleheads (above), and copperheads (below).

Jimmy Dunn, on his remarkable first solo ascent of a new El Cap route in 1972 (Cosmos), was the first to use copperheads for extended lengths on aid. Although the generic name is copperhead (a trademark of Bill Forrest), "heads" are made of both copper and aluminum.

Modern mashheads are generally home-made, and available from many sources. To determine quality, buy a Nikkopress gauge for a couple of dollars and make sure the swage meets sizing specifications (this will guarantee strength). Also make sure that the doubled-back wire just peeks out of the swage (if it comes out too far, it will fray and catch on slings). You can make your own Mashheads for about thirty cents each in materials, but a good swager costs around $150.

Sizing of mashheads: #0 (tiny), #1 (small), #2 (about the diameter of a cigarette), #3 (medium), #4 and #5 (aka cowheads – up to ½-inch diameter). The #0's have a cable that will just about hold the Holy Ghost and aren't really used much. Unless otherwise specified, a good spread would include 10 percent #1's, 35 percent #2's (a useful size), 25 percent #3's, and 30 percent of the larger sizes. Aluminum heads are generally used for the larger heads (#3 and up); they are normally more secure (especially in softer rock) than the copper articles. "Alumiheads" are not very durable, however, and often survive only one or two placements.

"Circleheads" are mashheads swaged into a loop. These are particularly useful for horizontal placements, as the pull is equalized on both sides. A few circleheads are generally all that you'll need for early ascents.

Copperheading Techniques

Like all difficult aid work, copperheading is an art, learned through experience. A well-placed head, especially in the larger sizes (#3 and up) can be very secure, and can occasionally hold a fall. To place a head, first pick the most appropriate spot, generally a shallow pocket or the recess of a corner. Clean out the placement by scraping with a knifeblade or the tip of a thin peg, so the head has a tidy area to stick to. Perhaps the head can first be shaped to the placement, accomplished by hammering it off to the side. First, lightly tap the head in place, then paste it in. A tool is frequently needed for the smaller heads (for larger heads, the pointed end of the hammer is often effective). Lost Arrows work okay for placing copperheads. I (J. M.) use a blunted ⅝-inch chisel (*never* for enhancement of the rock itself) tied to a long sling.

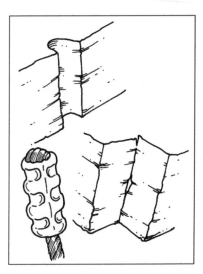

Copperhead pockets

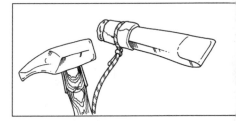

5/8-inch chisel

For most placements, the "X-em, paste-em, rock-em, sniff-em" technique is adequate. X-em: Imbed the head with multiple cross-hatched blows with chisel or piton; paste-em: pin the right and left side in; rock-em: hit the top and bottom and watch to see if it "rocks"; and finally, sniff-em, and "if it stinks, get off it!" In general, a well placed head will be pasted into every little undulation of the area around the placement. In extreme cases, I've (J.L.) placed two or three #0 heads within a few inches of each other, and equalized

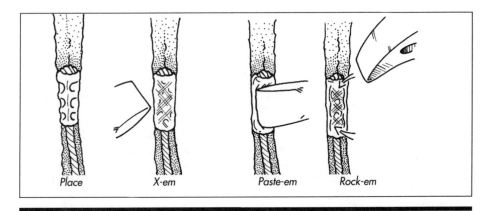

| Place | X-em | Paste-em | Rock-em |

them with hero loops. This is tricky and time consuming, but works surprisingly well.

Modern etiquette eschews the use of heads where a piton will work. Some trade routes have been ruined because climbers lack the ingenuity, or patients, to stack or tie-off pitons in shallow pockets. Heads generally get fixed, then tend to fray with subsequent ascents (attempts to clean them). So first try pitons, then resort to heading.

To remove mashheads, connect a sling from the copperhead to the hammer (having a hole in the hammer head simplifies this), and swing upwards, jerking it out. For some heads, a "funkness device" (a two-foot length of swaged cable, described in the "cleaning" section of Chapter 3: *Placements*) or a biner-chain may be required. It's considerate, however, to leave a copperhead fixed in place if it looks like the wire will rip out. Otherwise, an unsightly blob of metal will remain in possibly the only usable placement, and must later be tediously cleaned out by the next party. Trade routes generally have most heads fixed in place.

THIN NAILING

Thin nailing involves thin cracks or seams, and requires knifeblades, RURPs, and birdbeaks, which are thin, hooking type pitons. Aside from what's already been said, be particularly aware of those placements which "bottom out," (as most thin cracks/seams do). Overdriving a thin piton after it has bottomed out will only loosen the integrity of the placement. Birdbeaks are generally preferred in such placements. A RURP or two on the rack is still useful for horizontal thin placements.

Again, the principal error when nailing thin cracks is overdriving. Knifeblades will buckle and loosen; the beefier Lost Arrows will chip away the surrounding rock, and ruin the placement. This is even more so the case with RURPs, because the taper of the blade is so pronounced. Easy does it, for your own sake, and those to follow. Keep the tie-off loops close to the wall to reduce leverage. And remember to run a hero loop through the eyes of stacked pins so in case they pop, you don't loose the matrix.

A5 Birdbeak

EXPANDING PLACEMENTS

Expanding cracks and flakes can often present the most difficult aid problems. The risk is that each successive piece will loosen the piece that you're on, possibly causing it to fall out of the crack. Take care to note the difference between expanding and loose rock. Loose rock usually requires free climbing and/or hooking around the loose section, or extreme care if you're taking the loose stuff head on. Expanding cracks that accept camming units are generally no problem. But beware: cams exert more outward force on an expanding flake than do tapers and hexes, so go with the latter if the section is especially pliant and nut placements are obtainable.

Thin expando is tricky business. Always clip into the higher piece with a daisy. After Walt Shipley and I (J.M.) climbed a new route (The Kali-Yuga) on Half Dome, we renamed the monolith "Expandome," due to the majority of hard, expanding thin nailing on the exfoliating granite. On a A3+ knifeblade expando sandstone pitch on The Radiator, in Zion, several times the piece I was on popped as I was pounding the piece above, suddenly loading the daisy, and quickly finding myself secured solely to the untested piece overhead. Frightening. This is common on difficult expando, and requires a cool head and good timing per when to wail on the higher piece (which may soon be your only attachment to the rock).

Anything you suspect is expanding, check it out with a few gentle hammer blows. Beware of flakes that sound like a cheap cymbal. You're looking for a sound like the lower keys on a marimba. An echo or reverberation usually means the flake is hollow. Overdriving a piton at the start of an expanding section will often make subsequent placements more secure. The purpose here is to take most of the expansion out of the flake from the beginning. Be careful not to blow the flake apart, however. Try to alternate pitons with thin nuts (or hooks) if possible, understanding that pitons usually expand the flake more than cams or nuts. Aggressive bounce testing is not always recommended with expanding flakes, as it may expand the flake too much and spit out the whole works. In rare cases, you may have to free climb an expanding flake in which you can't set SLCD's. One trick that might work is to expand the flake by driving in a piton, slotting a taper or a hex in an appropriate spot, then cleaning the pin. If the nut is placed in a decent spot, where the flake pinches below it, then the increased pressure on the nut might help. If the nut is simply held in place by the pressure of the flake, don't count on it holding a fall. This technique can also be effective if used for the first placement on the flake, to get a sort of "protection" nut for the stuff above. Try it in the middle of an expando section, however, and you'll probably dilate the flake so much that whatever you're standing on will likely pop.

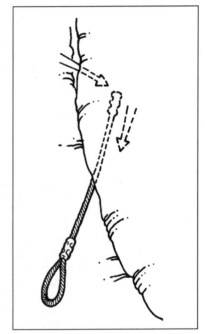

Expando copperheading

Expando copperheading is exciting duty. When a flake is too loose or too thin for pins, tapping copperheads deep into the flake (with a long knifeblade) and weighting them until they (hopefully) catch, is the technique. The copperheads act as stoppers, secured by the pressure of the flake.

CONCLUSION

Although we have broken down difficult aid climbing into several categories, it is impossible to describe every placement that you may encounter. A good aid climber will analyze each placement, and address specific needs individually. Each placement becomes its own puzzle, which is half the joy of aid climbing. Speed, efficiency and safety are the prime characteristics when making aid placements, but realize that when the going gets tough, it is best to take the time to be sure: one mistake can result in a whipper that requires hours of work to reestablish.

This was brought home to me (J.L.) when Richard Harrison and I made the first ascent of a steep climb on the Watchtower, in Sequoia National Park. On the morning of the second day, what we thought was a crack (when studying the wall through binoculars) turned out to be a thin quartz dike. There was nothing to nail, but by hooking and copperheading between little pebbles in the flaky quartz intrusion, I was able to make pretty good progress and avoid any bolts over the first sixty feet. But the placements were extremely marginal – many of them popped several times during testing. A5 if ever there was such a thing. Above, the dike blanked out, but there was a ledge and a good crack out left. A couple more placements and I could sink a bolt and pendulum over. But I got hasty, and eased onto a piano wire copperhead without adequately testing it; it blew out and I plunged down the wall. Amazingly, a big copperhead – thirty feet below – arrested my fall, or I would have zippered everything right back to the belay. The sixty-foot screamer wasn't so bad – I only got some scrapes on my right forearm – but having to renail the dike was grievous, and took hours. Test everything. Thoroughly.

Aside from what we have already covered, it is questionable if anything further will really help you on the high crag. Understand that the only real knowledge comes from experience. This is the limitation of writing about something that, aside from basic principals, is basically ad libbed. And that's the magic of wall climbing. No matter how many walls you climb, in some ways, each new one will seem like the first one.

First Ascents

During an ascent of the Pacific Ocean Wall, my (J.M.) partner Werner Braun commented on how the P.O. was the first wall to "cross the line into the absurd." The "line" we were crossing was somewhere between climbing a long, obvious, soaring crack system, and a nebulous, nearly invisible series of connected flakes and cracks (like those found on the P.O.) With all the obvious lines on El Cap now climbed, one can no longer sit in El Cap Meadow and spot the new, unclimbed line with the naked eye. Instead, binoculars and Celestron C-90 telescopes have become standard equipment, and the definition of a climbable line has, in turn, been redefined.

The modern wall climber, perforce, has a finer sense of what can and cannot be done. (This includes a sense of what is a reasonable number of drilled holes). Man's desire to climb new rock does not diminish with the absence of unclimbed, obvious lines; rather, the pioneering spirit remains as hot as ever. Only the gear, techniques, and attitudes change.

NATURAL LINES

A route's "naturalness" is determined by the number of bolts and manufactured placements required. There is aesthetic value in finding a natural line of features to ascend. It's pointless to drill one's way up a blank wall merely for an ascent. Chiseling slots for copperheads is just as contrived as bolting up blank rock, and these placements should be counted and tallied to determine the overall naturalness of the route. As it has always been, the modern game is to climb new routes that require minimum alteration to the stone's native state. Modern aid climbing has evolved in techniques, tools and skills to enable a route like the Wall of the Early Morning Light to go with far fewer holes than the 320 Harding needed twenty years ago.

First ascents require extensive planning prior to the actual ascent. This includes drawing a topo of the proposed route, determined by peering through a telescope and mapping out potential features and alternative features, which will give you some notion about the required gear. Generally, lots of extra equipment should be included to account for what cannot be determined visually. The "unknown," the prerequisite to adventure, is in abundant supply on first ascents.

Scouting for routes or scouting for climbers? El Cap Meadow on a big day.

Bob Gaines photo

Modern anchors in granite are normally fashioned with ⁵⁄₁₆-inch bolts. ¼-inch Rawl Buttonhead (1 ½-inch length) bolts are also still used on big walls. The Rawl hand drilling system is the historical standard and is still in use today. It consists of a holder (with optional rubber grip), a tapered shank drill bit,

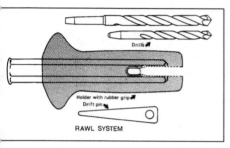

Drills

Holder with rubber grip
Drift pin

RAWL SYSTEM

and a drift pin (a wedge for removing drills from the holder). Commercially available drill bits are still popular, but the best is to modify inexpensive High Speed Steel or Cobalt Steel hardware store drill bits to fit the holder. For ¼-inch bolts and rivets, ¹⁷⁄₆₄-inch drill bits are the best (¹⁄₆₄-inch larger than straight ¼-inch). It takes only minutes to modify these for a Rawl holder. Taper the shank on a grinder so it fits in the holder on a grinder. Grind the tip to a chisel tip.

Rivets used for aid are: ⁵⁄₁₆-inch diameter, ¾-inch long, coarse-thread, grade 5 machine bolts that can be hammered securely in ¹⁷⁄₆₄-inch holes. Depending on the rock, some hammering or filing down of the rivet threads may be necessary.

Aside from these global comments, there is little more to add concerning first ascents. No amount of advice from this manual can compensate for a lack of experience and confidence. Perhaps the best thing I (J.L.) can say is to recall an incident that happened some years ago in the cafeteria at Yosemite.

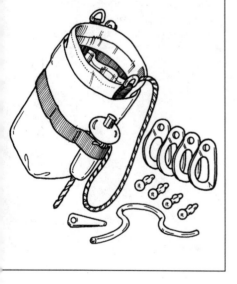

I was with Hugh Burton, a Canadian climber who was then recognized as a master wall climber. Only 24, he'd already put up several new routes on El Capitan. A younger climber came to our table and asked Hugh for advice about bagging big new walls. Hugh suggested that our visitor go to some scrappy area where nobody ever climbed and experiment on short routes first. After he felt comfortable on one-pitch routes, perhaps then the young man could move on to bigger routes. Our guest, who already had a catalog of big walls to his credit, scorned Hugh's advice. After all, he noted, the first new climb Hugh ever bagged was a grade 6 whopper on El Capitan. "True," Hugh stated, "but I didn't have to ask anyone how to do it."

When you're ready to start establishing new big walls, you'll know it.

CHAPTER 12

Solo Techniques

Soloing a wall can be a great experience. It's a unique adventure, testing the climber to his or her physical and mental limits. Soloing involves a tremendous amount of work, a high degree of commitment and uncertainty, and an intense amount of solitude. No one on earth is so alone as someone who is hanging in a hammock in the still of the night, half a mile up a big wall – alone.

Techniques are generally the same as with a partner, except that a self-contained belay system is required. For pure or mostly aid routes, the clove-hitch system works well. The climber ties a clove hitch in the lead line and clips it into a locking "pearbiner" on the harness. One end of the lead line is anchored into the belay (must be good for upward pull), and the other end can be left to hang (or tied in and/or backed up – tied in short to the climber – depending on to what degree the system is trusted. Letting the lead line hang single strand, however, prevents a loop from getting hung up on flakes. Slack must be passed through the clove hitch as each move is made. Having two pearbiners allows large amounts of slack to be had (for free-climbing) while still remaining tied in. Tie a second clove hitch in the second pearbiner with the required amount of slack, then untie the first clove hitch.

New mechanical devices now available greatly increase efficiency and ease of use with solo self-belay systems. Rock Exotica's "Solo-aid" device is essentially a mechanical version of the clove hitch, yet is a lot easier to use than a clove hitch, and is just as strong and secure.

One advantage to soloing is that rope drag is never a problem (the rope remains fixed in relation to the pieces); in fact, the rope can be tied into bomber pieces anywhere on the pitch. Leading and following pendulums is more difficult on the solo, requiring the use of jumars and/or a rappel device. Of major importance is setting up the haul line properly before beginning a pitch so that it doesn't snag while climbing. A rope bucket was designed for this very purpose, to allow a rope to be stacked in a hanging bag, and is essential for roped big wall soloing.

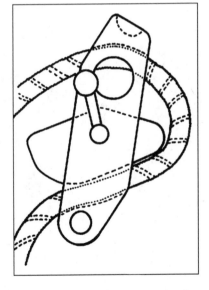

Rock Exotica's Soloaid

Once a lead is finished, the pitch must be rappelled and cleaned, and the bag hauled. A standard system entails rapping down the haul line (setting up the haul system

A solo hauling system that requires extreme care in setting up!

before rappelling – a third jumar or a self-contained hauling pulley is required), freeing the haulbag, cleaning the pitch, hauling, and setting up to lead the next pitch. Getting back to the previous belay can be difficult if the pitch traverses considerably; infrequently, two ropes must be tied together (must be set up before leading the pitch). One rope is then rappelled and the next jumared to the previous belay; the latter rope is then pulled back into the belay and used to lower out the haulbag. Generally, however, it is possible to simply rappel down on one rope and pull oneself (possibly with the jumars) back to the previous belay.

For straight-up pitches, the rappel/body haul system (the "sporty" system) can be used: two ropes are trailed in addition to the lead line: the haul line and a rappel line. The haulbag is left solely on a fifi hook (must be rigged properly so that an upward pull on the haul line will lift it off the anchor); the haulbag is then body-hauled as the pitch is rappelled. (Set up the haul system carefully so that no snags develop.) Though huge amounts of energy are saved, this system can be dangerous unless everything is set up exactly right. Of major importance is to leave the haulbag on a remote part of the anchor so that a fall while leading would not disrupt the haulbag's anchor, possibly causing it to fall (disaster).

A5 Rope Bucket

These are the basics. There are various other soloing systems, but rather than doing an exhaustive study of them, we have focused on the best and most proven of the many ways to do this exacting work. The only sane way to dial the process in is to practice the system on short aid routes, and slowly work into longer routes. We have intentionally left the topic of solo wall climbing rather truncated so the perspective soloer will start off small. Once you understand the basic belay system, it is entirely your own responsibility to go out and perfect the whole process. Too much talk in a manual like this can only confuse things, and perhaps give someone the idea that solo wall climbing is strictly a matter of technique. It is not. Try it, and you will quickly see why. A minimum of six big walls (with a partner) is prerequisite for trying one solo. Soloing even the busiest trade wall is twice as dangerous, three times the work, and four times as scary as doing so with a partner.

Style
and Ethics

Wall climbing's tradition is one of pioneers who utilized the best available technologies, developed new specialized tools, and brought to bear novel and strange techniques in order to ascend previously insuperable expanses of rock. When the austere hardman John Salathé and partner Anton Nelson first climbed the Lost Arrow Chimney in 1947, they introduced the notion of multi-day climbs, a radical departure from the traditional rock climbing style then prevalent in Yosemite. By the late '50s, the sheer faces of Half Dome and El Cap were still considered impassable, but the Robbins/-Harding era changed all that (and initiated the idea of "style" and its resulting controversies). By the late '60s and early '70s, wall climbing in Yosemite reached a peak under the hammers of individuals like Bridwell, Porter, Bard, Burton and Sutton predominating, each one a pioneer, each developing new methods and styles.

Presently, wall climbing has found some equilibrium, with the present game being to find those last great routes and to climb them with minimum bolting and rock sculpting. Other modern games include speed climbing (both of clean routes like the Nose, and nailing routes like the Shield), first clean ascents of nailing routes, and perhaps the boldest of all, no-bolt first ascents.

The future will bring new variations and refinements to the tournament, with new technology being influential, as well as leading wall climbers continuing to take the whole game to remote places like Patagonia, Baffin Island, and the Trango Tower area in Pakistan.

ETHICS

Wall climbing is a game whose rules are somewhat fluid; although a lot of climbers pretend to ignore their existence and refuse to acknowledge the unofficial canon, everyone draws the line somewhere. With walls, ethics grow from an individual's respect for the rock. Minimum impact becomes the name of the game. For first ascents, this translates to minimum bolting and riveting (never drilling unless absolutely no natural placement is available), and minimum rock sculpting (poor style in any case). For subsequent ascents, any altering of the rock (besides the unavoidable crack damage through placing and removing pins) is considered shoddy form. This includes drilling on lead (if you're drilling bolts where others didn't need them, you're certainly out of your league), chiseling the rock for better placements, etc. If

(opposite page)
The Great Trango Tower, Pakistan

Ace Kvale photo

climbers understand that the rock is a priceless and unrenewable resource, and that future climbers might well be scaling the same stone when our very bones are dust, the sport will remain in as good shape as we leave it.

SPEED CLIMBING

There are two reasons a team would consider speed climbing: because they want to, and because they need to.

The first mode is an expression of efficiency and, to some extent, athleticism; the second mode might save your life if you're committed high on some wilderness wall and are racing against heavy weather.

Flashing up walls has a long and storied history. In Yosemite Valley, the original test piece was the Steck/-Salathé route on the North Face of Sentinel. Throughout the '60s, various teams vied to shave minutes off the fastest time, culminating in Henry Barber's free solo, two-hour ascent in 1974. The following year, Jim Bridwell, Billy Westbay and I (J.L.) made the first one-day ascent of the Nose, on El Capitan, and speed climbing became immensely popular overnight. To many climbers, speed climbing walls is the

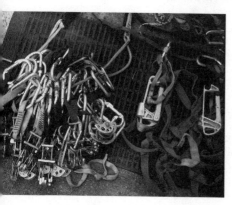

Nose-in-a-day rack
John Middendorf photo

ultimate expression of their skill and passion, and remains a fashionable style of ascent for those whose lives are centered around climbing. Perhaps more than anything else, in popular areas like Yosemite and Longs Peak, speed climbing walls allows present-day climbers the chance to do something new on routes that may have first been climbed decades ago; and defining themselves through new experiences is, and always will be, a vital characteristic of those on the cutting edge. Speed climbing should not, however, be construed as a requirement for every wall climber. It is specialized work, as we will see.

The first consideration is your partner. The criteria is different for speed climbing, where you don't share an extended amount of time together. Compatibility is a plus, not a requirement. The main consideration is that you can operate as an efficient team, which is principally a function of technical ability, experience, planning and communication. You don't have to like the other guy. You just have to be able to work together for a day.

Next is to pick the route. Definitions abound, but "speed climbing" usually refers climbing a route in one day, from bottom to top. (Fixed ropes are considered poor form, even cheating.) The first time out of the gate, crack off a small trade route so you can gauge your relative speed and endurance, and work out your procedures. A world-class climber might scoff at this recommendation, but it normally takes a few rapid ascents to discover your own pace and rhythm. Everyone and every team is a little different. And anyway, you're only talking about a day here, and if the warmup proves unnecessary, you still reap the thrills of polishing off a wall in a matter of hours. Once you feel confident of your abilities and have the system dialed in, you're ready to try to flash a Grade VI; and that's where the fun really begins.

First, evaluate the route. If you've done the climb before, sit down with your partner and devise a strategy. Most teams choose to break up the leading into sections, rather than swinging leads. The reasons are several. Following on jumars tends to go faster than following the pitch on belay. And speed jumaring can really smoke you. Consequently, if you've just blazed up a 150-foot pitch on jugs, you need a breather before jumping on the next lead, whereas the erstwhile leader has been resting. So study the topo, honestly appraise which climber is better at what technique (crack climbing, mixed aid and free, aid, etc.) and divvy up the pitches accordingly. If you haven't climbed the route before, ask around and find out all you can about problem areas – like nebulous sections of the route, weird belays, and so on.

An hour count to complete the route should be calculated and weighed against the length of the days. Figure the time for your descent into the equation, and tally it up. This will give you a good starting time. I'm not big on moonlight starts, but you might have to, and you'll want headlamps to get underway. Climbing with a headlamp is about three times slower than climbing in daylight – and ten times as scary. Figure this into your time estimate.

Since you probably won't have a haulbag, you'll need to carry a small day pack with your rations (the pack is worn by the climber jumaring). A two-person team should get by with a gallon of water for the day – more if it's hot. Tank up before you tie in. I like to drink a quart of water and a little juice before I get started. The tendency, owing to early starts, is to bolt down a thermos of coffee. Don't. Caffeine is a diuretic, and leeches the water out of you. Some teams like to spike the water with sports additives like Cytomax and Carbo-Fule. I personally go with straight water, and get the supplement boost from the food. Forget the hard vittles. Go with fruit and energy bars that are quickly digested and kick in fast. Anything high in glucose polymers will do. (This is not the venue to investigate the almost inexhaustible topic of sports nutrition, but if you plan on doing much speed climbing, you should familiarize yourself with the amazing energy supplements currently on the market. Energy bars are, in fact, probably the least effective of the many products available.) Load up on pasta, rice, spuds and yams the day before (carbo-loading). As for threads, descend in your rock shoes and avoid lugging tennis shoes. Consider bringing a couple sweaters if the nights are cool. Alpine/wilderness areas present individual problems relative to foreseeable temperatures and weather. If it's cold, go prepared, even if the pack is heavy.

Once you begin climbing, there are no rules whatsoever. Step on bolts, yard up on fixed gear – anything that will hasten the ascent. While it is sometimes faster to bash a piton in, they are almost always slower to clean, so use nuts whenever possible. Belays must be simple and secure. Unless the anchor is fixed, or readily accepts clean gear, I go with pitons as opposed to fiddling with, say, some elaborate equalization of a half dozen nuts.

Since one climber is leading a given section (usually at least six pitches consecutively), once the cleaner arrives at the belay, the leader must untie from the anchor (for the next lead) and tie the cleaner/belayer in. To quicken this transition, some teams prefer to tie into their harnesses with double, locking biners, gates opposed. This way the ends are quickly exchanged by first lashing both climbers to the belay anchor with a sling girth hitched to their harnesses, then unclipping the ends of the rope from the biner tie-ins and simply exchanging ends.

If tying into the rope solely with carabiners is worrisome, one may prefer the following technique to hasten belay switches. Instead of clipping off to the belay anchors with one carabiner at each anchor point, clip each anchor point off with two biners, and tie into the second biner. When the cleaner arrives at the belay, simply tie him into the first biner at each anchor point, have him put you on belay, unclip yourself from the second biner, and cast off. Here, you are simply tying the belayer off one biner below where you have been tied in. This system is fast, simple, and avoids having to tie into your harness with biners.

Appropriate gear selection is essential, not only for the overall rack, but also with what pieces you take for each lead. Pare down the rack, deciding what you need for the next pitch while the second is cleaning the previous lead. You should know exactly what you need before he arrives at your belay, so you can organize the rack quickly and appropriately.

Special equipment includes a longer than normal lead rope (180 feet) which will allow a leader to sometimes run two pitches together, thus eliminating a belay. Many pitches on walls are short, particularly if there are good ledges to stop at, and there are roofs and flakes that may make hauling problematic if the lead is strung out a full rope length. Running pitches together is normally faster, but not always. If you get to a ledge with three bolts, stop here rather than running the rope out and having to belay from slings higher up. Most teams opt to bring along a spare line (seven- or nine-millimeter) in the event of a forced retreat. The rope is usually carried in the daypack. Committing yourself to a big wall with only one rope is madness. In the event of a storm or injury, you're stuck.

A team's orientation and specific goals will determine the degree of risks they will take. With a few exceptions, I've never concerned myself with elapsed time, feeling that the main thing was to simply bag the climb in a day. For instance, on the first one day ascent of the Nose, I (J.L.) raced like a demon up the initial crack systems, often placing only one or two nuts for each pitch. When we got to the top of Boot Flake (about 40 percent up the wall), and realized it was only a little past eight o'clock, we settled into a nice rhythm and sort of coasted to the top, getting there with two hours of daylight left. Later parties started considering the climb as a race, shaving minutes off the fastest previous time because if they were to make a mark doing the same route in the same way, they'd have to do something differently.

In any event, once elapsed time became a popular concept (along with trying to climb two walls in one day), certain teams started simul-climbing (climbing simultaneously) over the easier stretches. It's hard to imagine something more dangerous than simul-climbing on a legitimate big wall, though the practice has only been attempted by experts and no accidents have (as yet) occurred. The notion is to keep the rope stretched between the leader and follower, with the leader periodically placing nuts that hopefully will catch the team if either climber pings off. I can't recommend this technique because it goes against my concept of mastery (an opinion that, perhaps, only I share). For me, flashing a big wall is making a statement, if only to yourself. The statement is that you are good enough to climb remarkably fast while maintaining complete control. I've never considered speed climbing a desperate act, rather a mental and technical accomplishment; sacrificing safety is not part of the equation. In fact, the real accomplishment is when you can flash a long route as safely as if you took a week to climb it. Then you're bomber, the practice is sane, and you're free to enjoy the mind-boggling rush of blazing up an ocean of rock without fretting your balls off about the consequences of a foot slipping off a hold. But tastes differ.

With that much said, I should add that when Dale Bard and I (J.L.) made the second one-day ascent of El Capitan (via the West Face) in 1976, we did virtually everything differently than what I have just advised. We had never climbed the route, didn't talk to anyone who had, didn't study the topo, and only vaguely knew where the route even started. We brought what we figured was an appropriate rack, and climbed with one nine-millimeter rope. And we swung leads the whole way. When we got to Thanksgiving Ledge, with only a few hundred feet of 5.7 chimneying left, Dale coiled up the rope and put it over his shoulder, I shoved the rack into the day pack, clipped it to a sling on my harness (so it would hang below my back), and we soloed off, gaining the summit just under five hours after starting the climb. But our lack of preparation translated to more than a few hazards on the climb. I got off route while working through a vague section at the two-thousand foot level, and had to crank off some sketchy 5.10 face moves about eighty feet out from my last nut. Not good. Much better to work things out in

advance, and reckon all you can about a route before heading up on it.

On routes that feature extensive aid, a team of three is preferred. The process works like this: one climber leads, and trails another rope. When the lead is completed, one climber cleans the pitch, as the other climber speed-jumars the free rope. The speed-jumarer trails a rope as well, which becomes, in turn, either the lead rope, or the rope the leader will trail on the next pitch. The speed-jumarer also carries a second rack, so the leader can cast off on the lead long before the climber cleaning the previous pitch hits the belay. There is the problem of switching ends that we discussed earlier, but once you resolve that, the result is that with this system, someone is leading about ninety percent of the time, and the climbing goes quickly indeed. This system has allowed one-day ascents of nailing routes that would otherwise be impossible with a team of two (and are nonetheless remarkable with three climbers). Unlike routes featuring mixed free and aid, or a predominance of free climbing, walls that are predominately aid require a different division of labor. You need an ace aid climber to do most of the leading, a skilled and quick person to clean (a special skill), and a super-fit climber to speed-jug the free line. And remember, even if you've got the best team ever, and have everything planned down to the last knifeblade, nothing will work out as it should if you don't keep things organized. This is especially the case for the person cleaning, who must keep the rack well organized, or precious time is lost at every belay in sorting things out.

Perhaps the stickiest problem of all is the business of passing other parties. The first strategy is to keep your eye on the route and go when others are not on it. This is almost obligatory if you're planning on speed climbing a big nailing route. If you're thinking you can sort of slide by another team at any old hanging belay – think again. The belays are so gear-intensive and the bags and various lines so many and so unwieldy that doubling the whole works – which you'll have to do in trying to pass another party – can involve almost unthinkable complications. Just wait till the route is free, or the other team is so high on the wall that they'll be off before you can catch them. On trade routes, you'll probably never find the route completely free. The best that you can hope for is that you can pass other parties where there are ledges for belays. It is always an awkward affair, and don't always presume that things will go without a hitch. If you're tactful, and explain that you will be hanging the other team up for no more than fifteen minutes, you can usually work things out amicably. Trying to hardass a team that's already on the route is poor form, and if punches are thrown, you deserve to get the worst of them. Remember, the party in front of you has the right of way.

Once the climbing is over, you must get down; and after blazing up thousands of feet of rock, you're going to be fried.

(opposite page)
Steve Quinlan cleaning on Tribal Rite, El Capitan.

John Middendorf photo

Just how well you fare depends, to a great extent, on your nutrition the day before, and during the route. If you've carbo-loaded the previous day and kept your carbs up during the climb, you'll probably just be exhausted, not ruined. And little of this has to do with what kind of endurance you have or how good a climber you are. It's a physiological fact that once you've depleted your glycogen (energy) stores, you'll hit a wall bigger than Half Dome, and your body will start cannibalizing itself for energy. You'll likely be dehydrated, because two quarts of water is way too little for what you've just done (though it's impractical to carry much more). Moreover, once the adrenaline fades, you'll be as sleepy as Father Time. For these reasons, extreme vigilance should be paid during any descent, however easy. If you're flat-out wasted, and are looking at an intricate descent involving moonlight rappels and dubious terrain, it's probably better to light a fire and hunker down for the night. Bring matches or a lighter.

OUTSIDE THE ARENA

We have used Yosemite big walls as a reference point in investigating wall climbing, and that is only natural. Yosemite walls are the most famous, and many of the universal wall climbing techniques were discovered and perfected there. But the fact is, Yosemite walls account for very few of those found on the big earth. There are desert walls, alpine walls, arctic walls, jungle walls, high altitude walls, and so on. While the general technical systems we've laid down are the same ones used in any area and on any kind of rock, different environments require particular knowledge and strategies.

This was never brought home to me more forcefully than when Jim Bridwell and I (J.L.) were hired to do the utterly jackass stunt of rappelling down the 3,400-foot face of Angel Falls for a now defunct television show. Both Jim and I had done long rappels before on rescues; just the previous year, Lynn Hill and I had set the world's record for continuous rappel (3,000 feet from a helicopter – another jackass stunt for another defunct TV show). The money was green and Jim and I both figured we were in for an easy time of it. We almost perished. Sure, we rappelled in the same manner we always had, used the same equipment, tied the same knots, set anchors in the sodden wall exactly like we'd done countless times on El Capitan, Half Dome, Mt. Watkins, and Sentinel. But our clothing was all wrong for the heart of the Venezuelan rain forest, and our instincts for weather were little more than worthless because we were not accustomed to the vagaries of gorilla monsoon. Several years later, when we trekked across Borneo, our awareness improved, but in fact I'd make another half a dozen extended forays into the jungle before I understood how to operate with some confidence and security. So the first consideration is to know the area. If you don't, enlist someone who does, someone who can dial you into the special demands of arctic, desert, or whatever the environs happen to be. It matters little that you're the world's greatest nailer if you don't know how much water to take, how to keep the leeches off of you, what kind of boots to wear, and all the rest. It is impractical for us to broach the many special concerns relative to climbing in Patagonia, for instance. The most we can realistically accomplish is to serve up the generic systems, and delve into details when appropriate. It is each individual's task to become familiar with the particular conditions and necessities of a given area.

Providing you go about your business as thoroughly as you'd rack the gear while cleaning a difficult aid pitch, you can generally calculate the risks with some accuracy, and conduct your business accordingly. And if we've conveyed anything else in this manual, it's that systematic preparedness is the starting point for every adventure. Look at the preflight checklist a pilot goes through before firing up the Concord, for example. Or consider what a sawbones goes through prior to doing a hip replacement. It is not so much to reiterate what the pilot or the surgeon might already know, rather to insure that the basic and proven systems are squared away so when the unforseen arises – as it normally does – the boss is free to deal with it soberly, without nagging doubts that his ass is covered with the primary life support systems.

Let's look at a specific case to bring this all into focus. Say you're going into an alpine area to attempt a new wall climb. You know the weather is brutally cold, and the wind strong. So you dress accordingly. From discussions with other climbers familiar with the area, and from reading anything and everything you can about past attempts/ascents of the given cliff, you know the rock is good, but the cracks tend to be shallow. From studying photographs, you can reasonably figure there is only one decent ledge on your proposed route, which is steep, and some ways to the left of a large and perpetual cornice on the summit from which stones and debris periodically rain down. These things you can realistically know in advance, and can prepare for. You cannot know the unforseen – the detached pillar on the fifteenth pitch, say, that requires some rerouting. But because of assiduous planning, you can only be defeated by the unforseen – the detached pillar – because you are clothed for the cold and the wind, have brought all the gear for bottoming cracks, have not been dusted off the face by rockfall from the cornice, and so forth. That is the trick. If you prepare for the foreseen, it will probably not defeat you. By predicting and preparing for what you will most likely encounter, you won't be driven off the climb prematurely, before you even get to the part that requires on-the-spot tactics. With any luck, you will have divined all that you will encounter before you ever tie in to the rope. But don't count

*Loose rock on Iron
Hawk, El Capitan*

Russ Walling photo

on it. And that, I think, is the real beauty of the game, and
the one characteristic that vitalizes all forms of true
adventure – that you can never know everything in advance,
that the outcome is never assured till you crawl onto the
summit. And only then will you understand why we call wall
climbing "the sport of kings."

As a closing note, let me add that anyone interested in big
walls should read the accident reports published annually by
American and European alpine clubs. This is sobering study,
for you quickly learn that the accidents that occur on walls at
least half the time involve very experienced climbers.

Surprisingly few mishaps issue from bad fortune (rock fall, for instance) or from unavoidable falls on difficult aid pitches. Only someone who has not done much aid climbing would claim that any and all aid falls can be avoided with a little better judgement. No leader will climb many walls without falling at some time or another. Even if your focus is perfect and you test every placement with textbook efficiency, a RURP or a copperhead is bound to rip out if you use these tools enough. Why? Simply because postage-sized pitons and little bits of copper and aluminum swaged to guitar strings are inherently flimsy and insecure, because you can test them and they might still ping out after you've been on them for several minutes, because even the greatest technical nailer is always hedging his bets and pushing his luck when the going is severe.

In the last analysis, it is impossible to know with absolute certainty if a marginal placement will stay put for the necessary time to place another one. Experience and instinct can give a leader a very sound feel for the work, but you never know for sure. So even the greatest aid climbers are almost certain to fall at some time. And yet, getting back to the accident reports, very rarely do these falls result in injuries that require rescues. The vast majority of accidents – involving both novices and world-class wall climbers – are instances when a climber or climbing team got caught in a storm that they were unprepared for. In Yosemite, for instance, climbers are often lulled into casual attitudes about El Capitan because this is California, after all, with sunshine and blue skies and short, warm nights. Then a thunder-shower closes in, the flanks of El Capitan become veritable spillways of cold mountain water, and anyone in their path is instantly soaked, and if not properly prepared, quickly becomes hypothermic and incapable of going either up or down. Learn from this. Underestimate one single thing about living on a big wall, and that one thing will catch up with you – if not the first time out, then certainly in time. In some aspects, wall climbing is a sort of war. Those who come prepared for the worst are usually the ones who never encounter it.

CONCLUSION

Our imagination often conjures notions about places and things that reality frequently falls short of. But wall climbing is one of those rare things whose scope and immediacy goes beyond our dreams. On the high crag, we feel our life acutely. Though the sun and moon cut across the sky, time melts into a taut present tense as we encounter ourselves moment to moment. We feel our life and death. We are fully awake. The rest of our life is like driving in second gear.

Appendix 1

CLASSIC YOSEMITE BIG WALL ROUTES

By no means is the following a complete list. It's merely a selection of well-known walls broken down by category. Of course, fine big wall adventures can be had off the beaten path – discover them for yourself. The "hard" routes listed below are extreme indeed, and attempting these without the proper experience is not only dangerous, but invariably means that bolts will be added. Moderate routes require a fair amount of experience. The all-clean and trade routes merely require tenacity and good judgement.

Getting Started – Short Aid Routes:

Direct South Face, Rixon's Pinnacle
The Stigma
Bishop's Terrace (roof)
The Folly, Left Side

All Clean (or Nearly All Clean) Routes:

South Face, Washington's Column V, 5.9, A2
The Prow V, 5.9, A2+
Leaning Tower A2
Lost Arrow Spire, Direct V, 5.10, A2
Half Dome, Regular Route VI, 5.9, A1
The Nose VI, 5.10, A2
Salathé VI, 5.10, A2

Current Trade Routes:

Lurking Fear VI, 5.9, A2
The Shield VI, 5.8, A2+
Mescalito VI, 5.9, A3
Tangerine Trip VI, 5.9, A3
Zodiac VI, 5.9, A2+

Moderate Nailing Routes:

Never-Never-Land VI, 5.10, A3
Cosmos VI, 5.9, A3+
Magic Mushroom VI, 5.9, A3+
North American Wall VI, 5.8, A3
Pacific Ocean Wall VI, 5.9, A3+
Tis-sa-ack VI, 5.10, A3
Liberty Cap, SW Face (Werner's Woot) VI, 5.10, A3+
South Face of Half Dome VI, 5.9, A2+
Tribal Rite, El Cap VI, 5.10, A3+

(opposite page)

Sue McDevitt on the Direct on Half Dome

Dan McDevitt photo

Hard Nailing Routes:

Iron Hawk VI, 5.10, A4
Zenyatta Mendatta VI, 5.9, A4
Jolly Rodger VI, 5.11, A5
Sea of Dreams VI, 5.10, A5
Sheep Ranch VI, 5.10, A5
Atlantic Ocean Wall VI, 5.10, A4
Native Son VI, 5.10, A4
The Kali-Yuga (Half Dome) VI, 5.10, A4

Appendix 2

BIG WALL GEAR CHECKLIST

Big walls are gear-intensive, but it's possible to get started on the big stones without having to mortgage the house (if you can improvise here, and borrow there). If two climbers both have a standard free-climbing rack and decent camping/bivy gear, they already have about seventy-five percent of the total gear needed for a moderate nail-up, such as Mescalito, Zodiac, or the Shield. The following is a basic checklist of the gear required.

Hardware
(SFG stands for standard free climbing gear)

2 to 3 sets of Friends (SFG)
2 to 3 sets of wired stoppers (SFG)
2 to 3 sets of small brass-nuts (SFG)
80 carabiners (SFG)
Hook selection (2 to 5 of the standard types)
Copperhead selection (10 to 25)
Pitons (5 to 10 knifeblades, 10 to 20 horizontals,
    15 to 25 angles)
Small bolt kit (optional)

Personal Wall Gear (per climber)

Harness*
Aiders*
Jumars
Hammer and holster
Headlamp
Rain gear
Wall boots*
Kneepads and fingerless gloves
Wall spoon and Swiss army knife
Sleeping bag and ensolite

Other Stuff

Haulbag*
Portaledge*
Double gear sling*
Ropes (2 to 3)
Tie-offs and runners
Pulley
Stuff sacks for gear/food organization
Accoutrements, including first aid kit and repair kit
Food and water

The items on the checklist marked with an asterisk could be improvised. A portaledge, for example, can be anything from a plywood sheet rigged with cord or a suspended Kmart lawn chair, to the deluxe, manufactured portaledges now available. The harness can vary from a simple 2-inch swami and 1-inch leg loops to a custom-made padded wall harness. Aiders can be knotted from 1-inch web, or sewn. For wall boots, a sturdy pair of tennis shoes is adequate (bring free climbing shoes, too). A duct-taped duffle bag may suffice as a haulbag, or regular backpacks can be used to haul gear (a good, well-manufactured haul-bag made from abrasion-proof materials, however, is worth the investment). Two gear slings can be sewn together (with a speedy stitcher) for an adequate double gear sling. Be creative.

Sue McDevitt jugs on El Capitan.

Dan McDevitt photo

Appendix 3

NORTH AMERICAN BIG WALL AREAS

Yosemite

Yosemite is the big wall paradise. Good year-round climbing, long and aethestic granite routes, and accessible approaches make Yosemite the ultimate training ground for big routes. See Appendix 1 for list of routes.

Guidebook: *Yosemite Climbs: Big Walls,* by Don Reid.

Zion National Park, Utah

Zion is the new Yosemite, with an abundance of sandstone big walls, ranging from 600 to 2,200 feet in length. Seasons are short (in the spring and fall); summer temperatures can be roasting, while winters are generally cold and windy. Permits from the park service are required for any ascent requiring more than a day. Request a backcountry permit with exact details of the planned ascent at the Visitors' Center. The Visitors' Center is also home to two volumes of semi-organized notes, comments, topos, and route information on most of the established routes in Zion. There is no published Zion guidebook.

Recommended starter routes: Touchstone wall (C2), Spaceshot (C2+), Prodigal Sun (C2), and Moonlight Buttress (C2 or 5.12d). Recommended nailing routes: Lowe route on Angels Landing (V, 5.9, A2/3), Birdbeak Spire on the Sentinel (IV, 5.10, A2).

El Trono Blanco
(Sierra Juarez Mountains, Baja, Mexico)

For a 1700-foot big wall in a remote, wild place, El Trono Blanco is the finest. The remoteness becomes clear after the approach is made (though only a few miles, it takes an entire day to descend to the base). Either a guide or someone experienced with the area is required to find the turnoff to the starting point, which is close to the ghost town of El Progresso. The wall has many fine free routes, including the classic Pan American aid route (V, 5.9, A3). The testpiece is the Giraffe (V, 5.10, A4).

Wind River Range, Wyoming

The Winds has several good big walls, but the premier monolith is Mt. Hooker (1600 feet), requiring a 20-mile approach from Big Sandy to Haley Pass. Routes: The Robbins Route (5.10, A2, or 5.12), The Third Eye (5.10, A4).

Guidebook: *Climbing and Hiking in the Wind River Mountains,* by Joe Kelsey.

Black Canyon of the Gunnison, Colorado

The "Black Hole" is an intimidating and wild place to climb big walls. Once the descent is made into the 2,000-foot canyon, the commitment required in the area is well felt. Many of the routes go free at a high standard, but good aid big wall projects still abound. Recommended routes: Hallucinogen Wall (5.11, A3+) on North Chasm View wall, and The Dragon (5.10, A4) on the Painted Wall. No published guide, but the visitor's center has some route information.

Red Rocks, Nevada

Though mostly an excellent free climbing area, Red Rocks has some interesting big aid walls, most notably on The Rainbow Wall (1500 feet). Classics are Desert Solitaire (5.10, A3), Sargent Slaughter (5.10, A3), and the Original Route (5.9, A3).

Guidebook: *Red Rocks Select,* by Todd Swain.

Longs Peak, Colorado

The East Face of Longs Peak, The Diamond, is generally regarded as a haven for long alpine free climbing. It still offers some half dozen good aid climbs, including the Jack of Diamonds (A4), and the Dunn-Westbay (A3).

Guidebooks: *Climber's Guide to Rocky Mountain National Park,* by Richard Rossiter.

Whitesides Mountain, North Carolina

This 700-foot wall offers a few good big wall type routes, notably The Volunteer Wall (A4), and Blarney Stone (A4).

Guidebook: *The Climber's Guide to North Carolina,* by Thomas Kelley.

Cannon Cliff, New Hampshire

Cannon has some fine aid lines (notably The Ghost, A3) for East Coast climbers wanting to sharpen their aid skills.

Guidebook: *Rock Climbs in the White Mountains of New Hampshire,* by Ed Webster.

Appendix 4

SUPPLIERS OF BIG WALL EQUIPMENT

A5 Adventures, Inc.
1109 S. Plaza Way #296
Flagstaff, AZ 86001
(602) 779-5084
The big wall supply shop, supplying single and double portaledges, haulbags, Rope Buckets™, aiders, daisy chains, haulpacks and a line of big wall accoutrements

Boreal
(714) 361-8818
Big wall boots

Fish Products
(818) 355-8296
Portaledges, haulbags, and Fishhooks

Mountain Tools
(408) 393-1000
A complete range of products by mail order

Rock Exotica
(801) 292-1044
Hauling pulleys and other hardware items

Wild Things
(603) 356-6907
Aiders and daisies

Appendix 5

American Alpine Institute (aid seminars)
1212 24th St.
Bellingham, WA 98225
(206) 671-1505

Jackson Hole Mountain Guides (seminars)
P. O. Box 7477
Jackson, WY 83001
(307) 733-4979

John Middendorf (big wall excursions)
P. O. Box 236
Hurricane, UT 84737

Portland Mountain Guides
(seminars, big wall excursions)
P. O. Box 1462
Beaverton, OR 97075
(503) 641-2739

Vertical Adventures (seminars)
P. O. Box 7548
Newport Beach, CA 92658
(714) 854-6250

Yosemite Mountaineering School
(seminars, big wall excursions)
Yosemite National Park
Yosemite, CA 95389
(209) 372-1244

Glossary

The following is a compilation of some of the technical terms and jargon used throughout this book. This is a strictly American glossary; Brits, the French, or Japanese undoubtedly use somewhat different terminology.

A5 Adventures: a manufacturing shop which makes specialized big wall equipment for cutting-edge ascents.

aid: using means other than free climbing to get up a section of rock

aiders: step ladders made from webbing for moving up on aid placements.

alpine style: a method of big wall climbing which does not involve fixed ropes; the opposite of sieging

aluminum head: an aluminum swage on cable used for bashing into incipient grooves. Also see mashheads.

anchor: a means by which climbers are secured to a cliff

angles: pitons made from bent steel to fit cracks from 1/2" to 1 1/2" wide

artificial climbing: archaic term for aid climbing

ascenders: mechanical clamps that cam onto a rope and slide up, but not down, a rope

baby angles: the two smaller (1/2" and 5/8") angle pitons

back clean: to remove a previous placed piece of gear while climbing

bathook: a small pointed hook that is set into a shallow drilled hole; used in place of rivets, dowels and bolts for climbing blank sections of rock. The two most common bat hooks are the Leeper pointed and a ground down Black Diamond hook.

bashie: similar to a mashhead, but generally more block-shaped

belay: procedure of securing a climber by the use of a rope

belay seat: a wood board rigged with slings used to sit on while belaying

bight: a loop (as in a bight of rope)

biners: see carabiners

bivy, or bivouac: a place to sleep overnight

birdbeak: a hook-like blade piton manufactured by A5 Adventures for thin seams

blade: short term for a knifeblade piton

bolt: an artificial anchor placed in a hole drilled for that purpose

body-hauling: using your body as a counterweight to haul heavy loads

bomber or **bomb-proof:** absolutely fail-safe (as in a very solid anchor or combination of anchors)

bong: a large angle piton (2-inch to 4-inch) for wide cracks

bugaboo: a thick knifeblade piton

buttbag: a fabric seat used to make belays comfortable

cam: usually used to refer to camming type protection devices, also the part of the device which lodges against the rock

carabiners: aluminum alloy rings equipped with a spring-loaded snap gate; sometimes called biners or krabs

cheater stick: an extending pole to which a carabiner and slings are attached; used to skip past placements to clip fixed gear

chicken bolt: a bolt degrading the original character of a pitch placed by a subsequent ascent team who found a section of the climb too bold

chock: a wedge or mechanical device that provides an anchor in a rock crack

chockstone: a rock lodged in a crack

Chouinard hook: the previous name of the Black Diamond hook

circlehead: a copper or aluminum swage on a loop of cable used in horizontal placements

clean: a description of a route that is free of the need to place pitons; also the act of removing gear from a pitch

cleaner biner: a carabiner that is used to clip to pitons prior to removing them

counterweight hauling: a two-person haul system where one member of the team acts as a deadweight on the rope

copperhead: a cylindrical copper swage on cable used for incipient grooves (also mashheads or heads)

crux: the most difficult section of a climb or pitch

daisy chain: a length of webbing or cord with clip in loops along its entire length used to connect the climber to a placement

dihedral: an inside corner of rock

dowel: a short aluminum rod, hammered into a drilled hole, found on older climbs only; new climbs use rivets in lieu of dowels

drag: usually used in reference to the resistance of rope through carabiners

expanding: used to describe a block, crack, or flake which flexes or moves under the load of aid placements

exposure: the relative situation where a climb has particularly noticeable sheerness

fifi hook: a flat open hook fastened to a harness used for resting on placements

Fishhook: a large skyhook

fixed: gear or ropes left in place

free climbing: to climb using hands and feet only; the rope is only used to safeguard against injury, not for upward progress or resting

French free: resting on gear while climbing without aiders

funkness device: a short length of cable with a loop at both ends, used for cleaning purposes

gobis: hand abrasions which reflect poor aid technique

gear sling: sling used for carrying gear around the shoulder

hammer: tool used to place pitons and heads

haul: term used to describe the work of getting the gear up a climb

haulbag: bag used to drag equipment up a climb

haul line: rope used to haul the haulbag

headlamp: battery operated light attached to the head

heads: short term for mashheads

hooks: steel hook-shaped devices that are set on edges and knobs; available in many brands and styles

jumar: a type of ascender; often refers generically to any type of ascender or the process of ascending a rope

jugging: ascending a fixed rope with ascenders

knifeblade: a thin blade type piton

keyhole hanger: a bolt hanger modified so that it can slip over rivets and bolt heads

keeper sling: a tie-off sling used to secure a tied-off piton to a carabiner

lead: to be first on a climb, placing protection with which to protect oneself

lead line: the rope used for leading

leapfrogging: removing the previous placement and placing it again above

Leeper hooks: small hooks manufactured by Ed Leeper, available in flat and pointed styles

Leeper pitons: a piton with a Z-shaped cross-section manufactured by Ed Leeper; also called Z-tons or Z-pitons (out of production)

Lost Arrows: forged steel pitons, available in 8 sizes, distributed by Black Diamond (listed on topos as LAs)

lower-out line: rope used to lower the haulbags out on traversing pitches

line: the path of weakness in the rock which is the route

mashheads: cylindrical copper or aluminum swages on cable for hammered placements in incipient grooves (also copperheads or heads)

move: one of a series of motions necessary to gain climbing distance

nail: piton

New Wave: in modern aid climbing, generally used to denote difficult aid climbing involving extreme danger

Nikkopress: manufacturer of the swages used for mashheads

nut: same as a chock: a wedge or mechanical device that provides a secure anchor in a crack in the rock

peg: piton

pendulum: to swing across a rock face suspended by a rope

pin: piton

pitch: the section of rock between belays

pitons: metal spikes of various shapes, hammered into the rock to provide anchors in cracks (also pins, pegs, or nails)

placement: a nut or anchor in the rock

portaledge: originally coined by Mike Graham, now a generic term for hanging platforms on which to sleep

pulley: used for hauling

protection, or pro: the anchors used to safeguard the leader

prusik: both the knot and a means by which one ascends a rope

rappel: to descend a rope by means of mechanical brake devices

Rawldrive: a split-shank contraction bolt

ring-angle claw: a large homemade hook bent from old ring angle pitons

rivet: steel machine screw hammered into a shallow drilled hole

rivet hanger: swaged cable loop that is used to cinch over rivets and hangerless bolts

rope bucket: a bag for stacking the rope, manufactured by A5 Adventures

RURP: realized ultimate reality piton; a thin, postage stamp-sized piton

RP: the original brass nut, sometimes used generically for small silver soldered nuts

second: the second person on a rope team, usually also the leader's belayer

sieging: leaving fixed ropes on a climb to facilitate the ascent and descent; generally considered a lesser form than alpine big wall climbing

skyhook: see hooks

sling or **runner:** a webbing loop used for a variety of purposes to anchor to the rock

sling belay: a hanging belay with no stance; listed as SB on topos

soft iron piton: soft, malleable pitons that are generally not reusable

stacking: wedging two or more pitons in a placement; also refers to a method of organizing a rope

stance: a standing rest spot, often the site of the belay

stoppers: generic term for wedge-shaped nuts

supertape: the thick 9/16" or 11/16" tubular webbing, with 2500 lb tensile strength, not the thinner 9/16" web

swage: copper or aluminum cylinder used for connecting cable

swager: a press used to make mashheads

tension traverse: climbing sideways with the aid of a rope

tie-offs: short loops of thin webbing that are hitched over a piton used to reduce leverage; pitons with tie-offs on them are "tied-off"

topo: a map of a route

top-stepping: standing in the highest rung of an aid ladder

traverse: to move sideways, without altitude gain

wall or **big wall:** a long climb traditionally done over multiple days

zipline: a small diameter (generally 7-millimeter) rope carried by the leader in lieu of a haul line, used to stay connected to the belayer

zippering: falling and ripping out many pieces in a row

Climbing is Dangerous: Stack the Odds in your favor.

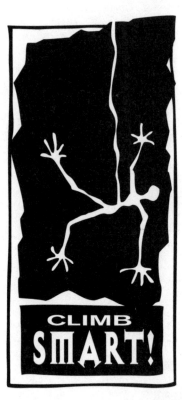

CLIMB SMART!

- Check your knots and harness buckle
- Inspect your gear and replace as necessary
- Know your partners and their habits
- Check your belay—are you sure you're on?
- Read all warnings—they can save your life
- Fixed gear is unreliable—back it up when possible
- Keep an eye on the weather
- Rock breaks—check your holds
- Always double check your rappel system

--Remember-- your safety is your responsibility

Climb Smart! is a public information program of the Climbing Sports Group, the trade association of the climbing industry.